Middle Ages

Ages

A History From Beginning to End

(An Enthralling Overview of the English Middle Ages)

Bertha Pereira

Published By **Jordan Levy**

Bertha Pereira

All Rights Reserved

Middle Ages: A History From Beginning to End (An Enthralling Overview of the English Middle Ages)

ISBN 978-1-77485-723-6

No part of this guidebook shall be reproduced in any form without permission in writing from the publisher except in the case of brief quotations embodied in critical articles or reviews.

Legal & Disclaimer

The information contained in this ebook is not designed to replace or take the place of any form of medicine or professional medical advice. The information in this ebook has been provided for educational & entertainment purposes only.

The information contained in this book has been compiled from sources deemed reliable, and it is accurate to the best of the Author's knowledge; however, the Author cannot guarantee its accuracy and validity and cannot be held liable for any errors or omissions. Changes are periodically made to this book. You must consult your doctor or get professional medical advice before using any of the suggested remedies, techniques, or information in this book.

Upon using the information contained in this book, you agree to hold harmless the Author from and against any damages, costs, and expenses, including any legal fees potentially resulting from the application of any of the information provided by this guide. This disclaimer applies to any damages or injury caused by the use and application, whether directly or indirectly, of any advice or information presented, whether for breach of contract, tort, negligence, personal injury, criminal intent, or under any other cause of action.

You agree to accept all risks of using the information presented inside this book. You need to consult a professional medical practitioner in order to ensure you are both able and healthy enough to participate in this program.

TABLE OF CONTENTS

Introduction

If you listen to anyone talk about the Middle Ages as a general notion, you'll be hearing them describe it as a time period that occurred between two very popular periods that is the decline of Rome and the start of the Renaissance. For a long time, historians looked at this period of time as Middle Ages as an average moment in our history, and as a period of no importance. The reason they believed this was the fact that nothing was invented or discovered during this period in comparison to the times that followed it. Up until recently it was believed that the Middle Ages were remembered for the terrible time between 1347-1350, when there was a Black Death swept through Europe and killed 20 millions of people.

What we know today about we know that Middle Ages was a vibrant period and deserves attention for the many events which should be recounted. This book we'll explore the lives of the people who lived in during the Middle Ages and how their lives were lived in the period. There are many new discoveries waiting for you when you decipher from the popular portrayal of what was known about the Royal Family and the true portrayal based on the facts uncovered by historians. There is not much that we can reveal about the lives of individuals and go deep into time to the Viking Age and observe the basic lives of the people who lived in the countryside during this period of the course of. Learn about the lives of the people who comprised this period of time known as the Middle Ages in the upcoming chapters.

Chapter 1: The People Of The Middle Ages

The middle ages of life is like a fairytale particularly when you watch it on the numerous TV shows that attempt to portray it. But should you venture into the past of the middle ages you'd get a shock surprise. The reality of life was not as straightforward and enchanting as the movies portray and those living in the era were fighting a lot to maintain a sense of normalcy.

At first, women were generally mistreated. There was no respect for their thoughtsand opinions. Many thought that they did not have the capacity to do anything. That's why the ladies who stood out during this period are highly valued, because they set the standard.

There was also disease. Plagues, also known as black death were all over the place and they were fearful. Other diseases were also linked to hygiene, which led to vermin and other diseases. The result was deaths on a large scale, often destroying whole communities. If disease didn't take a life, it is probable that a fight could. There was always a battle or other taking place.

To ensure the survival of civilisation, there were savage rules implemented. These included torture, murder or even witchcraft to punish offenders. Devastation was commonplace, as was being held on an edifice at the peak of a huge tower. In some instances prisoners were imprisoned underground in dark and cold prisons, which were guarded by guards.

Despite all the difficulties of the past there were many people who were able to live throughout the middle age. Through this publication, you'll be able to learn about the lives of a few and how people lived, as well as their convictions.

Saint Nicholas
Many people are familiar with the great saint Nicholas because he is immortalized in our culture as a big man who was wearing white and red with a gray beard. What they don't realize is his legacy that he left behind during his time in the Middle Ages and how he became an icon in our books on history. The legend of Santa Clause was derived by his initials, Saint Nicholas But nobody knows the events that led to this sort of fame.

Prior to his time that he slid down the chimneys St. Nicholas was the bishop of Myra and served in the reign of Constantine the Great. It was around the time of the 4th century. There is a an mention of him in the writings from the sixth century under Justinian's reign. Justinian and this has led to numerous questions. Are they the same saints who is being mentioned? A lot of people believe that the reference to him in the sixth century some way only references to his tomb, and that many believed that the oil derived from it could be healing. There are also stories and rumors suggesting that tell stories of miracles occurring due to St. Nicholas's tomb.

St Nicholas was initially connected with the sea and not with Christmas or the celebrations that occur at the close of each year. He was Bishop of Myra The city of Myra was not just Myra an ocean port, but the church where he was a priest was situated over the original Temple of Poseidon. Poseidon according to the story by the authors of Greek Mythology, is the God of the seas, and is the son of powerful Zeus. According to legend, Saint Nicholas magnificently shook Poseidon's temple

Poseidon and placed him in the position of all those who traveled the oceans. The saint was praised with offerings. saint to ensure secure travel and calm waters as storms were threatening.

The most well-known account about how saint Nicholas discovered his connection to the holiday season when three daughters were spared from prostitution. In the days of poverty, was rampant, when parents were no longer able to provide their children with food or sell them to prostitution or slavery. Saint Nicholas recognized that this family was starving for food, and to ensure that the children from being taken into slavery or abusing, he threw bags full of gold in the windows of their home to stop this from occurring. Saint Nicholas grew into an image of patronage, handing out money to those with no money, and distributing gifts to his followers.

In the latter stage in during the Middle Ages, there became St Nicholas Day that was celebrated on the 6th day of December. It was a day of joy full of gifts and celebrations. American writers, Washington Irving and Clement Moore and others, among others, invented the Santa Clause in the past 100 years or more. While Santa Clause's White horse is now replaced by reindeer and a sleigh the customs of giving gifts and patronage remain to Saint Nicholas of in the Middle Ages.

People from during the Middle Ages: Knights
The term knight or "knight with shining armor' is widely made up over the many years. The term "knight" nowadays is a result of performing some kind of saving act, however it's possible to say without doubt that these acts differ from the original rules of business. There's been a time when women have called the man as a knight to help them manage their food or changing a wheel on a vehicle; this is in stark contrast to the way knights were viewed back in earlier times. Middle Ages.
In during the Middle Ages, a knight was a soldier in armor who was regarded as courageous and noble. Nowadays the term knight is used to describe anyone who has been awarded honourary title, but who does not have to participate in any conflict or protect their country. We've seen films of the soldiers in silver armor, riding on horses in

combat. This is the real thing of a knight as it was a soldier in armor who rode on horseback. The term "knight" was associated with a high standing in the society and a degree of nobility, most likely due to the expense of getting the right armor.

Knights were able to, theoretically confer a knighthood upon those they believed to be worthy. It was, however, an honor to receive a knighthood at the hands of the monarch. In order to ensure the advancement of knighthood to social status there was a code of conduct that was required to be put in place, as did an appropriate dress code to reflect their status as noble. Gold spurs and belts of white were the standard of dress for knights. This ensured uniformity. it was not disputed, since everyone felt a great sense of respect for being given this dress. Alongside uniformity, knights were required to swear allegiance to a Lord of the country. They were actually soldiers and were relied upon to the Lord to be ready to go to assist him.

When knights first came into the picture in the middle of the Middle Ages, they acted as bloodthirsty warriors and displayed an aggressive streak. This caused a lot of concern and rulers worried that they would not be managed and could cause havoc across the kingdom. An order of conduct was enacted by the Catholic church, and it was the one responsible for this. The church recognized it was becoming apparent that knights became disruptive; they intervened and established an order of conduct that the knights had to follow. They called them the knightly virtues', and they helped bring harmony to the chaos that they had created.

The virtues include:

Mercy is only extended to those in need. It was uplifting to the Knights to not show mercy to those who committed crimes and could have a negative impact on the land they guarded

Humility

Honor

- Sacrifice

"Fear of God

- Faithfulness

Courage

Women deserve respect of all ages in the society

The virtues they exemplified were important and were adopted in the course of time and to the satisfaction of the church. Knights' role in society transformed dramatically during the tranquil times in the Middle Ages and when longbows were introduced. Knights were employed for hand-to-hand combat and also used swords to fight. After the introduction of arrows and, later, guns were introduced, the utility of knights diminished. Through peaceful times and as late as in the sixteenth century, knights were able to be employed for entertainment during tournaments. These events required an extensive amount of training and skill, however, they were very different in comparison to the bloody fights that they initially fought in. The tournaments cooled in the course of time since they began as a mock battle where knights were expected to battle to the death on the battleground of a stage. With time, they evolved into one-on one combat we've seen on the screen.

Like everything else were gradually fading out of fashion, and knights were further removed from the battle. They were now regarded as only people of nobility and status. It is not easy to tell the way they looked in the early Middle Ages. Knighthoods are still in use throughout the countries listed below:

The United Kingdom

- The Netherlands

-- Malaysia
- Denmark
The current knighthoods don't necessarily involve honoring their combat service. Males are now able to receive an honorary knighthood for their dedication to in their professions, like literature or music. Paul McCartney from The Beatles is called Sir Paul McCartney in recognition to his contributions to the world of music. The female version of Paul McCartney is Dame and was awarded to people like Dame Helen Mirren for her activities in the entertainment industry.

People from in the Middle Ages: Vikings
Pop culture has accurately represented the Vikings as fierce and skilled sailors who sacked the coastlines in England, Ireland and a large portion of Europe between the 8th and the end of the century. The appropriate name is'ship-born warriors'., Vikings were originally from Scandinavia and firmly established their place in history through the title Viking Age from their actions in the 9th and 8th centuries, as well as 10th and 11th century.

The Viking Age earned its name due to their impressive battles throughout the period. From seemingly disadvantaged background they Vikings were able to conquer river and shores from Europe, Ireland, Great Britain, Normandy, the Shetland, Orkney and Faroe Islands, Iceland and Greenland. They even reached North America in what is now Canada, Maine and Massachusetts.

Viking is a word that means pirate in Norse and this relates to the way they gained new territories, as they would approach it by the sea and then take it with skilled force. In the past, they were known as savages, and while they did attack villages and took to seas, the majority of Vikings prefer farming as a means to earn enough money to live. Their ability to navigate the seas comes from their mastery of woodworking. From Scandinavian trees , they constructed famous long boats, cargo vessels and the feared Dragon Ships.

While they were branded savages, Vikings were also adroit in their legal system with "law" being an Viking word. Their practices could be primitive, including the use of a dual in order to settle the case and juries to render the verdict of the defendant. Sometimes, they used an instrument to discern the innocence of a person, that first blood drop that would fall was the one of the person who was guilty. They believed that the gods will always be in favor of innocent and would not allow the drop of blood get released. It is not surprising that this kind of decision-making method was eliminated after Christianity was introduced to Scandinavia.

Clothing

Much like the rest of world in the Middle Ages, wool was preferred for clothing and was the first choice for the Vikings. Vikings were known to sail with sheep to ensure they could have clothes during their time at sea , conducting raids. Like in modern times it was women who made the clothes. After taking the wool from the hair of sheep, they would make use of minerals and vegetables to dye the clothes, and white or cream would draw excessive attention.

The most common attire for men Viking would be long pants and a long-sleeved shirt constructed of wool. The pants were kept in place by some sort of belt that took the shape of drawstring. Leather boots and socks were a necessity because of the cold climate out at the sea. Additionally, they would wear layers to keep warm from cold weather, which made them appear larger in stature. Incredibly, the average height of the average Viking was moderately five feet eight inches. While it is not exactly average in modern times, this height allowed the Vikings surpass the smaller Europeans they met.

Religion

Important to keep in mind, Vikings did their actions and lived in accordance with the predictions of one of their gods. Contrary to the other Middle Ages, Vikings only changed to Christianity at the end of the 12th Century which was quite a while following that of the Viking Age itself.

Here are a few of the gods who guided the Vikings in the Viking Age:

Odin Odin Vikings were of the belief that, after their death they would be buried in Valhalla in the place the home of their gods. Odin was the ruler of Valhalla and was considered to be as the God to gods. Odin was also known as the God of War poetry, wisdom, and magic. Anthony Hopkins recently portrayed him in the adaptation of the film for the Thor film franchise. As he appeared in the film, Odin only had one-eye and legend has it that Odin sacrificed his eye for the source known as the fountain of knowledge,

Mimir. Odin was believed to be the most powerful among all gods and was feared by the Vikings even before Christianity was introduced to Scandinavia.

Loki known as a tricker and a trickster, the Vikings frequently blamed Loki when things went wrong or went against the plan. Loki defeated Balder God of joy and light and is referred to as the giant that symbolizes evil. A god with a lot of knowledge, Loki possessed a strong understanding of the world, and his savvy often enabled him to trick gods to perform his deeds. Vikings were of the belief that Loki could take on the evil forces in the final battle to bring about the all times.

Hel Goddess of the Dead and child of Loki, Odin threw Hel into Niflheim. She was ruled by her father and received many powers from her rule, also called Hel. The word "hell" came from the goddess and is used to describe the realm of the dead.

Thor was adored to the Vikings, Thor was the most powerful in the Aesir and is still revered as the god of thunder. Thor is derived from the Germanic word meaning Thunder and is typically represented as lightning bolts. The weapon he uses is as well-known as his name. When surrendered, the mighty Hammer of

Thor could trigger lightning bolts. The picture of Thor is a tall man with a beard of ginger.

The Valkyries Maidens who fought to serve Odin The Valkyries were famous for their judgments on fallen warriors. Based on their actions in combat, they decided their fate. A lot of Vikings believed that the Valkyries could decide if you would be alive or not in battle and the fate of your life would be determined before the battle had even began.

The Viking Raids

Vikings were superior to other people of Europe due to this, their actions were feared by this period of the Middle Ages. England is the very first nation to be invaded by the Vikings in 793. They invaded a monastery, and caused some to question their relationship with God. What is the reason we are being attacked? Could it be because our faith isn't enough? Or did we do something wrong?

Due to their high quality of their workmanship their vessels were able to dock in places that others couldn't. The reason for this was the aspect of surprise? It was impossible to predict the next location they would strike and it was not worth protecting ports or locations for entry since they could dock virtually everywhere. They didn't venture into the inland areas and mostly attacked coastal towns. The reason for this was a couple of reasons. First, they could strike without warning, and take villages off guard. Additionally, they could transport more directly into the boats, without having to transport it for miles. In addition, with the sleek and modern design of their boats they were unable for anyone to pursue them at sea. If they moved further into the inland waters, they could be pursued by foot.

There was a lot of debate about why the Vikings chose to attack numerous nations in the Viking time. Vikings didn't believe that there was a afterlife and, as such they wanted to establish themselves in the history books while they were on the earth. Social status was extremely important to them, and to be regarded as powerful and unbeatable warriors was their primary aim. The Vikings were avid fighters and considered it an enjoyable way to spend their time constantly engaged in fight.

In addition to their faith in the Valkyries they believed that the date and time they died was already set and nothing they could do would alter this. Therefore, they carried out extremely risky actions without fear because they believed that it wouldn't alter the date of their death since it was already set. If you were to imagine yourself as the thought of a Viking and scout villages, they'd be in no danger since when they were hurt they were the ones to blame and not the actions of their comrades. It was an extremely freeing way of living as well. Vikings are remembered as such.

It was the End of the Vikings

The Viking Age saw its end in 1066. There are many theories about the events that led to the closing of the raids however superior weaponry for defense is the main theory. As the strength of Europe increased and their defenses grew, so did their strength and castles. It's much more difficult to attack a village that is with moats and sturdy walls if you don't have the appropriate numbers or weapons. Another event that brought about changes was the death of the King Haraldr from Norway. Following his death, Norse influences over Europe decreased steadily. There is a popular belief that the spread of Christianity into Scandinavia is the cause of the end of the Viking Age. Gods of war such as Odin and Thor inspired Vikings to adopt the values and morals associated with the

Christian faith. It would help them move in the opposite direction.

The Christian belief system holds that if you do your best to people around you and proclaim the power of God as your Lord and savior, you'll have a safe route into the next life. Christianity also introduced the belief that there is a life beyond death. This was that was not previously believed in the time of Vikings. Their traditional way of living in the Viking time period did not allow them being allowed to pass through to the Holy Gates and into heaven.

People from in the Middle Ages: Women
Women were considered to be inferior in times of the Middle Ages and had seemingly no influence in the making of decisions. Despite their lower status, women were often have a lot of expertise and would not stay jobless. The majority of women were poor and were forced to do all day long in a gruelling environment to earn a living to provide for their families. While society prefers that women be heard and not seen The influence of women in their time in the Middle Ages is greatly underestimated. Behind every King of this time was a strong, powerful woman.

Women's rights were greatly restricted in those days. Middle Ages and men could use them as they wanted. Women were forced to submit if she were not in line with their husbands or masters because disobedience was viewed as unfaithful to God. Women weren't to be ignored, and many women are remembered because of their heroic actions in this period of the Middle Ages. Most likely the most well-known, Joan of Arc, continues to be featured in current Pop Culture as an icon for women empowerment and feminist movements.

Joan of Arc

Born around 1412, in France At 18 years old, she was able to lead her fellow French into victory over English. Joan said she had visions that gave her knowledge of the best way to save France. She demanded an interview together with Dauphin and admitted to knowing how she could save France and regain the crown and the right for the throne of France away from England. Charles the Dauphin was always skeptical however he reacted after she gained her popularity among the villager.

He gave Joan an armory and horse and let her go to battle in Orleans. There she took an active part in winning France before returning back to Charles as victorious. She then urged the new ruler to make an appearance at Reims to be recognized as the real ruler. The King and his advisors were wary however, they soon reacted to the idea and, on July 18th day of July 1429, he was made as King Charles VII. It was recorded the fact that Joan herself was awed by the King during the ceremony.

A year later, Joan was captured during an encounter after being thrown from her horse. The Burgundians held her in captivity while they engaged in negotiations with England to get a substantial part of the money she owed. The English considered her valuable since she was the instrument of France which led to their victory. England paid her 10,000 francs and promptly put her in prison in the midst of trial. Charles VII decided to distance himself from her and make nothing to see her released.

The English called her an heretic, and then burned Joan in the courtroom following an unconvincing trial. It took over 500 years before she could be made a saint in the status of an Roman Catholic, but this was the case in May 16th, 1920.

Noblewomen

The majority of women believe that women in those days of the Middle Ages had no rights and were merely a slave to the dictates and wishes of men. However, this is not the case however, if we can rank the severity of treatment according to their social standing Peasants were often able to live an easy life, without any hardship. Women, however, were required to follow men and follow their orders without arguing with their authority. If they followed the guidelines, women were not always punished, especially noblewomen. Noblewomen achieved the status as nobles by marrying well or having been birthed into the status.

They had responsibilities, and were required to manage household personnel and, obviously their children. Making sure that their children were educated was the responsibility of the wife, and the level of education the children received directly reflected on her and the condition of their home. If the home fell into an unintentional state as it was in the past and the blame fell on the wife since she was responsible for assign the servants in a way that would keep the house in good order while husband was off to his business.

Noblewomen were often the ones to care for sick people and occasionally the poor when they felt inclined. Being more entitled than women with lower standards, they were to suffer the death of a family member or of her spouse, a noblewoman may even inherit land, and thus be the legal owner. In charge of the household and their troops could be sent to battle under the direction of women. When the spouse was not involved and the lord wanted the deployment, it was her responsibility to dispatch the troops needed.

Chapter 2: The People Of The Middle Ages: Minstrels And Merchants

Merchants

The term is now used to refer to business owners or entrepreneurs, merchants of those days in Middle Ages traded in all kinds of commodities to earn a decent income. They would establish their own stall or shop in the town, just as vendors are today in pop-up market. The most sought-after items that were sold at the beginning were iron, salt and textiles. It was the first product and demanded some level of expertise to purchase and market these things. Items that were rare, like spices and silk, were difficult to find as they were sourced directly from China or from the Middle East. You'll need to be connected to the world of trade to obtain the items you need to sell.

As with all things there is competition, it grew continuously and the demand for finest, most rare of products grew stronger. A small group of highly skilled crafters rapidly grew, and they were referred to as craftsmen. They didn't have to sell the products, but their talents were sought after to make unique items which were later sold by traders at a greater cost than the standard offerings on the market. Artists could make shoe, cloth, or even glasses. It is not surprising that these items would command a greater cost than salt. The rise of artists, and, more specifically sculptures, who created decorations for homes with the most expensive.

Women were usually the ones who came up with the ideas behind these products like cloth and shoes. They were the ones who weaved and usually run an e-commerce of their own , employing ladies to help show others how to weave in order to increase the sizes of orders. The most desirable person could be a traveler who frequently bought precious pieces from remote locations which were impossible to find in the city. Noblemen will pay a premium for something unique that no other person could own.

Merchants' Perception

In the case of merchants it is important to think about the people who are using their services to determine their perspective. In the middle age there were three types of people which could be seen in the community. There were peasants, fighters and clergy. According to peasants and the clergy, people who were merchants weren't beneficial to the society.

They were viewed as being a wealthy squatter with no regard for anyone else.

From this view point The clergy were not happy with the business practices that merchants were engaged in, particularly in relation to banking and trade. They even went so far as to inform the citizens of the vicinity that merchants were ignoring the direction of God. The outcome was that should there be any incidents or mishaps like natural disasters, merchants would be the ones to blame. They believed that they caused God to be punished.

When you look at the viewpoint of merchants, you see an entirely different perception or picture. They believed that merchants were viewed as misers, people who refused to spend the money they earned. The merchants were thought of as being calculating, making a point of calculating their earnings as well as the losses due to their job.

Merchants also fought for themselves which is why there were many battles between them. This would happen in the trade routes which saw merchants who were mostly Venetians and Genoese fighting for buyers. On the routes they would trade in spices, perfumes food, and silk. Those who controlled the trade also gained an advantage.

In the social order the position of a merchant was over a peasant due their ability to travel, trade and earn huge amounts of money. In the following decades, they became the most influential and rich individuals in the society.

Minstrels

Businesses independently Minstrels were entertainers who moved from village to village in small groups. They were able to earn money and they traveled in large groups with other entertainers. The most popular type of entertainment were jugglers, dancers, and acrobats.

It's impossible to undervalue the value of minstrels to society. When they first began their journey they were criticized by the church. the minstrels completely because they offered entertainment that appeared to be sexual in nature. This was reported in poetry. As time passed the minstrels were more well-known, because they were keeping records of their performances and national literature. The more civilized the society became more diverse, the more varied the subject matter of the songs were. In addition, the instruments were used also became diverse.

Minstrels could be found in both royal families and also among people who weren't part of that noble category. People who were not noble would travel from one town to the next and entertain the inhabitants of the villages. People awaited the minstrels' visits because there was nothing other entertainment.

-

When it came to various minstrels, there were certain levels they could aim to achieve. One of those levels includes the Harper. When the time was the Saxons they were musicians and provided entertainment at celebrations. To find the most talented minstrels in the world, the harp would be distributed throughout the room, letting various people would play. While they played there was singing being performed.

The person who was the harper is considered to be very notable. He would read the music composed by him, and play it to the guests who were waiting for him. There were also a huge range of instruments performed by other minstrels such as the lyre and cymbals, flute, organ , and the viol. To play more upbeat music carillons were used, which are also referred to by the name of hand bells.

In the royal court there was a certain minstrel that stood out from the other performers. He was called"The King of Minstrels and was recognized for being the best of all other musicians.

Many names were used to describe them all over Europe However, they were adored by the public for their happiness and entertainment.

Music Types

There were many kinds of music performed by minstrels. This included the following:

Sacred Music

Minstrels could also perform worship in the most sacred manner through music. They were mostly found in houses of noble families and were often heard playing prior to dinner being served, or during the evening prayers prior to the serving of supper. If there were guests living in castles there would be a ceremony conducted by the chaplain, and the minstrel would assist to play the music necessary to bring the service ahead. There were occasions when congregation would sing psalms and then minstrels would play the instrumental accompaniment.

Dinner Music

At the time, right before dinner was served, the servants would arrive with dishes, while minstrels play music. After the food was served the music would go on while minstrels entertained at the table.

Apart from playing music, they be able to tell stories of romance to guests, or inform them of their background. In the majority of these cases the minstrels would be in a chair on the floor, or, in some instances they'd be seated on the table.

People from in the Middle Ages: Religious Persons

Bishops

Bishops, like the ones we have today, were appointed to head the church and served to God as well as the Pope. In contrast to today, in order in order to be a bishop one needed to first be a nobleman. A bishop's role was similar to an owner of a business, and they had to oversee the nuns and priests and monks as well as oversee all the administrative duties that the parish had to perform. This isn't something that happens nowadays The church would often have large areas of land in different areas of Europe. There were even knights under their command, and, during the beginning of the Middle Ages, they were commanders in battle, and were in the front line to advance their knights.

Priests

The priests were under the direction of the authority of the bishop and spent their lives following his directives. They offered spiritual guidance to the people of the town and led services and organize religious ceremonies for the congregation at the church they resided at. Priests, just like bishops, would devote their entire lives in preaching message of God and to preserving their Christian belief in the community.

Monks and Nuns

Monks were men , while Nuns were females. They were committed to their faith and be required to surrender everything material possessions they owned to spend their lives as worshippers. They would reside in convents, as well as monasteries. At the time of Middle Ages, monks and nuns also worked as nurses and doctors, and also cared for the sick and old. They lived lives that was simple, spending their time in prayer and devotion to their faith. They would not have a spouse or husband since this was not allowed. A significant portion of their lives were devoted to the care of those in need in the city their convent or monastery was located in. This could mean to provide food or clothing or to simply preach the gospel of Jesus Christ and assist the less fortunate people to further their studies in Christianity.

Friars

In contrast to nuns and monks, friars had no place of residence and would travel the world preaching the message of God. They also devoted all their time to the cause of their faith but they would find the non-believers and convert them to Christianity by preaching as a single person , rather than in a congregation. They did not receive any compensation for their work and frequently depended on the generosity of others. Some actually begging to survive. They also believed that they had to preach their faith to those who were less fortunate, and not only to a city They would venture out to the farms and give sermons to those who didn't have access to an organized church.

People from in the Middle Ages: Kings, Queens, and Vassals

King

In the eyes of pop culture They Middle Ages are famous for their castles, kings as well as the Royal Family. The king ruled over a vast area of land, and was expected to protect the land and ensure the best living conditions for his subjects. As one can imagine the task of governing the vast expanse of land is difficult and challenging to manage. The king then gave vast amounts of his estate to local lords of his choice. The lords who were vassals were and were extremely important in the eyes of the King. As a reward for their generosity the king demanded his vassals to support his requests if they ever needed this in battle. They were totally loyal to him, and would fight whenever he requested to do so.

To understand the kings of the middle ages, it is necessary to know the period that they reside in. There are three periods, which include the middle age, high middle ages, and the final middle times. In the early middle ages kingdoms were being created and at the same time, there was an increase in technology as well as an increase in yields from crops. In the middle of the times, there was a war via Magyars, Vikings as well as Saracens. These are the notable medieval kings.

King Harold II

The King Harold II of England received recognition for one reason, even though it may not be the most prestigious place. He fought William the Conqueror, and lost to his Norman forces at the Battle of Hastings. The battle lasted for an entire day. It was over with the death of Harold II, the King Harold II was killed in the eye by an bow. This was the shot that caused his death and the complete destruction of his troops. According to Anglo Saxon kings go, He was the last of England.

Alfred the Great

Out of all the Kings of middle times it was the only one that was called The Great. He was frequently referred to as a gentle man because he wasn't the most vicious warrior, but he thrived in the administration field instead. He was educated by the cleric because the age of his four brothers. It was the demise of two brothers that set the ball into motion for his eventual accession to King. Along with his third brother, he assumed the role of chief adviser and counselor as king. He also helped his brother to win in battle against the Saxons.

The brother of the deceased began to become sick, and his condition worsened until he passed away leaving his son, who was just a baby. This led to Alfred becoming the king for a total period of 28 years. Every campaign Alfred fought during his reign , he was successful. Based on the foundation that was created his son, and later their grandson managed initiate with the Saxon Reconquista of England.

Frederick Barbarossa

The year was 1122 when the Kind was born and he lived to when he was 68 years old. He was crowned King in 1152, and later Roman Emperor at the age of 1155. He was famous for launching the third crusade along with English King Richard the Lion Heart and a French King called Phillip Augustus. In this crusade, he had an army of over one hundred thousand soldiers, with twenty thousand of them were knights. He died when he considered traversing the Saleph River on horseback instead of crossing the bridge that was in use. The river's current was so strong that when he was wearing armor, he drowned.

Henry II, King Henry II

The King Henry II served as the King of England between the years 1154 to 1189. While he was king and in control, he was able to bring order to the amount of power the barons enjoyed. He attempted to do the same for the courts of the church to restore an orderly state, but he could not achieve this after the death of Thomas Becket. Becket. Thomas a Becket served as the Archbishop of Canterbury in 1170. His successor was later his son Richard I the Lionheart.

Richard the Lionheart

Richard I was a King of England and reigned for ten years, from 1189 to 1199. He was also known by the name of Richard the Lionheart He was an interesting route to the throne as his ascendance to the throne followed the deaths of two brothers. The name was given to Richard the Lionheart for a number of reasons, including his capacity to be a mastermind in the military. He was a fascinating person and displayed humility in certain times, but very arrogant in other times. He was brutal in his battles with his adversaries and they loved him.

Vassals

As we mentioned earlier they were lords that were given vast areas of land by their kings as a reward in exchange for loyalty. The land they received was referred to as fiefs and could be turned into towns that were their own. The vassals were able to run their fiefs as they saw they wanted and also assign areas of their property to other vassals. It was a privilege to be able to run your own fief. And in the present, we could have called them mayors , if mayors owned the land and oversee the land.

Queens

The media has frequently portrayed queens of the Middle Ages as baby-makers who served as accompanists for her king during any royal appointment. It's not true and queens of their time in the Middle Ages had a very crucial role to play within the monarchy as well as in society. If a monarch was in a state of illness or was too young to make crucial choices, the queen would be the regent and take on the responsibilities of the monarch. Queens were relied upon to make wise choices.

The duties of a queen

Like today's politics There was a lot of concealment and secret in the Middle Ages.

The monarchs were always at risk of being sacked by their enemies or allies, therefore it was crucial to stay at a step in front of your adversaries to ensure your position on the throw. One of the duties of the queen was to come up with innovative methods to spy on their adversaries and get as much information about their plans as she could. Because women are often on the streets, engaging in conversation and chatting with friends, the queen would employ spies who would bring back any information that she might transmit to her King. The majority of gossip also came from the queen. An crucial tool for igniting conflict was to spark gossip that spread throughout the land and get to listeners of enemies.

As queen, she'd have to assist her husband to plan his strategy and frequently assist him in analysing messages from other leaders, and understand the significance in the messages received. A king always trusted his queen because if they would fall, and her too, and, together, they'd be able to protect each other. The queen was also the only person a monarch could be with on his own. In the past, accompanied by guards or servants, kings could be assured that there were no spies or conflicts in ears when they were alone with their queen.

In movies, we often observe the queen in the castle by herself for long periods of time but, in the fact that queens accompany their kings everywhere. Because they were part his circle of friends the king would want to ensure that his Queen was as near as he could, in case they needed her.

The most significant duty the queen was required to perform was to provide male heirs to carry in the monarch's legacy. To ensure the throwing and to ensure its security, the king had to ensure a legal male successor. This could result in the pressure being heaviest on the queen as she is the one who would maintain her husband's control over the throw. The first child she had would be considered as the one most significant since if she was incapable of conceiving an heir to the throne who was healthy the queen was often shunned or even executed. The divorce was not commonplace and was extremely feared since it was against the beliefs to divorce the couple from anything except death.

Queens were also required to play the role of hostess , socialite, and also be the ideal host for the stream of guests who frequented her home. They were accountable to make guests feel comfortable at their residence and making sure an enjoyable time throughout their visit. The guests could be allies, or even potential allies who had to be convinced from the family of the monarchs. They also served as glorified party planners, having to coordinate many banquets, banquets, and feasts. Their manners and intellect had to be perfected because they were often with the king on his international trips and also served as women's representatives for their empire.

Seven Queens of England Seven Queens of England

Similar to the monarchs of England There were seven queens that stood outand are referred to in the tradition of"the Plantagenet Queens. They were:

The king of the world, Eleanor from Aquitaine The King Henry II was on her the throne from 1154 until 1189. Her personality was notable for being a strong personality. She was the one who was in charge of her sons and led them in a battle against their father during a rebellion Her most prominent children included Kings John as well as the King Richard I.

The queen spouse to the King Richard I was referred to as the Queen Berengaria from Navarre. She was a king between 1189 and 1199. With Richard the Lionheart as her husband You can be certain her to be a determined woman who gave him a lot of assistance. One thing that people often people will mention is the fact that she loved her husband deeply. When he was abducted and held from the King of Austria She took every step in her power to pay the ransom in order she could secure back to freedom. One of her regrets was the fact that she didn't have any children that could take over the throne.

The next queen to succeed her was Isabelle who was the daughter of Angouleme. She was the queen's concert for the queen John and was the queen's heir between 1199 to 1216. While this queen didn't be a part of many events at the period she was a witness to several of these. Her official title was Queen Consort of England She also had one child , who later became the King Henry III. She was present to witness the Barons revolts and when the Magna Carta was signed. Magna Carta and the Legend of Robin Hood.

the fourth queen is referred to in the title Eleanor from Provence. She was the wife to the king Henry III who ruled between 1216 to 1272. One of the most notable characteristics of the monarch was the beauty of her, that was noticed by all who came across her. She was extremely loyal to her husband throughout her time in office. She was there during the time that she was present when the English parliament was formed as well as witnessing the battles between Simon de Montford.

The queen spouse of King Edward I was known as Eleanor of Castile and was on the throne from 1272 between 1272 and 1307. She was the daughter of a king , and was later married to an heir to the throne. She isn't remembered as much for her achievements as she is remembered by her death. In the event of her death there were crosses that were erected by her husband to ensure to be remembered. They are referred to in the form of Eleanor Crosses. But, in her life time she was a witness to the Battle of Scotland which was fought in opposition to William Wallace, John Ballot and Robert Bruce.

"The She Wolf of France was the name was her name by many, even though her real name was Isabella from France. She was the consort of King Edward II, and spent her time in the throne between 1307 and 1327. Her mother was King Edward III. Her memories are contaminated by negative incidents. In the beginning she was not faithful to her husband , the king and was involved in an affair Roger Mortimer. In the middle of her affair and was able to come up with plans to murder the king. The plan did not succeed. actions could be justifiable in some cases since her husband was in a sexual relationship to Piers Galveston.

7th Queen was wife to King Edward III and was known as Philippa of Hainault. She was king up to 1369. The last queen of this list had an extensive family, giving birth to twelve children. Although she gave her husband an impressive family but he was recognized for his sexy ways. She was alive at the start of the Hundred Years War, and she died from the Black Death.

People from during the Middle Ages: Peasants It's possible to be astonished as what is the definition of a peasant. It's not always one who is homeless or who lives day-to-day with a small amount of food and cash. A peasant is a person who lives in a rural area and is able to work with others or tend to their own farm. They could even rent out business properties or even own the place themselves. They were considered to be a minuscule compared to the nobles and women however, they were self-sufficient and hard-working people. The peasants relied on cultivating their own land and would work all day long to give their families to be able to live comfortably. They were often referred to as the labor force employed in agriculture of during the Middle Ages.

Peasants comprised the majority of the population. This could have a positive impact on the ruler of a specific town. In contrast to urban dwellers, peasants were extremely conservative and loyal even to the point of being a bit naive. They rarely questioned the law and were extremely meticulous about maintaining a solid connection to God in their churches. The peasants were not able to challenge the current power structures , and although they lived more modestly than nobles, they rarely complained and went about their lives. Urban dwellers are typically quick to ask for more and constantly try to improve their standard of living.

The societies that were comprised of peasants had a strong social network that was supportive of them and often had to depend on one another in times of stress. Help was always offered and it was not uncommon for a peasant to aid with a neighbor who faced difficult times. It could be in the form of a harsh climate not producing enough food to meet the demands of the season, and the chief of the household passing away with the wife and children left with no money. The loyalty of the peasants was robust and outsiders were not received with open arms as the were usually considered to be very close and close.

Peasants didn't have their own leaders, and usually there was an established order within an organization of peasants. The leader was chosen by the peasants and typically was their representative when they were called upon to express their opinions.

Prior to the advent of the concept of cash, peasants had been content with living on the bare minimum and never felt the desire to increase their wealth. They generally lived off the land and harvested the benefits they needed, and had no desire to increase the amount of work in order to generate a higher quantity of output. The peasants lived on a minimum wage and were very different from urban dwellers who were constantly seeking to raise their living standards.

As we look back some would consider this method of living as lazy and insipid. However, if you consider it what is the reason they would produce more food than their family could eat? If they were not growing with the purpose of selling the harvest, then why would they do they need to increase their labor to produce more food that can be eaten? The term "peasant" is often mentioned as a form of insult. This is usually the case when people are slammed for calling someone the rural labourer. They might have been the lower classes however, they were hard-working people who cared about their possessions and lived off their personal property.

People from that time period. Middle Ages: Children

If we look at the lives of children in to the Middle Ages to that of the present, we would be able to see a huge difference as children had a limited amount of freedom during the past. Our children are able to take advantage of the outdoors and have a leisure time without the pressure of advancing to the age of marriage or an age at which the work ethic was accepted. The tasks we do today aren't as great as the expectations of children at the time.

The concept of class is extended to kids, too as they were judged as a group based on how much they were superior biologically. Children were born noble , or born as peasants It was extremely difficult to alter according to society in the event that one was born in a particular class. The law at the time provided that childhood could be enjoyed from beginning of the birth period until the age of 12. Even though they were still very youthful, an infant who reached twelve years old was thought to be competent and competent enough to be accepted into society. Additionally the possibility of girls being married at the age of twelve. Boys had to wait until fourteen to marry their brides.

Being as a part of society at an early age and this also entails with a lot of responsibility, since they were considered adults should they commit crimes. Children were frequently utilized to strengthen bonds with their families. weddings arranged by a couple were extremely popular , and weddings were just equivalent to a formal agreement between wealthy families. The arrangement of marriages was also extended to the royal families. In many cases queens would only be becoming women when they were married to their monarchs.

Chapter 3: Some Famous Persons Who Were Famous In The Middle Ages

The Middle times featured a wide amount of both women and men who became famous or were famous and unforgettable simultaneously. Here are a few famous people of the middle ageswho came from all walks of life.

Marco Polo

He was born at the the middle age in the Venice Republic. The son was a businessman who held significant influence. It was together with his father, that he traveled across Asia. As time passed his father and uncle encountered the Kublai Khan, and through them, they gained powerful positions in the monarchy.

At the age of 21, he was old, he landed the position of an envoy for the ruler of China. After a while, he was awarded an increase in rank and was promoted to governor. He decided to travel to Venice and, during his excursion, he was detained and sent to prison in the Genoese prison. He compiled a book of his experience in travel, and wrote"The Travels of Marco Polo" "The The Travels of Marco Polo".

Dante Alighieri

In Florence Italy in the year 1265 There was a writer called Dante. The term "writer" is just scratching the top of what he was capable of. In addition, he is a theorist , whose ideas are still being considered until the present day. He was also the first to introduce to the political realm. Additionally, he was also philosopher who was focused on ethics as well as the aspects of morality.

Ivan the Terrible

Ivan was both royalty-bound being the grandson of a Grand Prince called Vasily III. He was living in Moscow as well as the child of the second wife of his father.

Ivan Was a person who was interested in power and was a man who pursued power with enthusiasm. As a mature and was the one of the first to get honored to be the Tsar of Russia. He was the first to hold this title and the reason for his title was due to the fact that he gave the title to himself. In the Tsar title, the belief was that his power came directly from God.

Ivan the Terrible was also known under other names, such as Ivan Grozny and Ivan Vasilyevich. He was a war hero both in Poland in Poland and Sweden and was mostly unsuccessful.

Vlad the Impaler

If you think of the myth of Dracula and you think that it's all simply a myth. But you're wrong since during the middle ages there was a person who is believed to be the inspiration for the story of Dracula. Vlad is believed to have been born Vlad Tepes in 1432 in Transylvania. His father was called Vlad Dracul and is name was associated with the devil. Vlad Tepes was called the impaler because the meaning behind his name was impaler. The name was perfectly with his personality since he was famous for the murder of many thousand of individuals. He was known to have killed many people, with some saying the number at 20,000, while others believed that the number could have been as high as 300,000.

If he could get ahold of his captives and tortured them, he'd do it to perfection. He perfected his method of torture by ripping insects apart and watching them decay slowly. Sometimes, he'd impale them. He was not afraid of using his new abilities on others, and then watching them slowly die.

He used to torture his victims for fun and gave him great happiness. A thing he was most famous for was to make his victims lie down on a stake that was extremely sharp. The more important a person was, the more important the stake constructed. After their death, Vlad would leave the individuals to die in the open. The scent of their corpses would affect all the others, while he appeared in no way in any way.

Robin Hood

Robin Hood is known for taking money from the wealthy and giving it to the poor however, he was more than just a bandit. He began as an Norman noble, but over time, he transformed into an outlaw. To survive and help the people close to him, he resorted to locating people who could reach him and then stealing from them. The reason he did this was because he believed they had plenty of money to spare. There are those who claim that the archer employed bows and arrows when fighting in his crusades. Some have also said that they believed that he was a cold-blooded killer who had a desire for the blood of the royals.

Chapter 4: Famous Stories From Medieval Times

The medieval characters do not just include those living and, but also those who had fascinating experiences. There are characters in stories that continue to live on throughout time and will never disappear. There is a chance that the stories are based on facts, but as a all, they're fictional. Here's an example of one the more well-known stories from the past.

Hansel and Gretel

This is a tale of the woodcutter who was poor and lived in a tiny cottage located in the middle of an area of forest. The house he lived in had two kids, one boy and one girl who was named Hansel as well as Gretel. He didn't have his former wife with him, thus he arranged to marry another woman to assist him in raising his family. The woman was brutal and treated the children in a horrible way. Additionally she was able to spend a large time pestering the woodcutter. Consequently, everyone in the household was affected. Her main complaint was over food, because she felt that there wasn't enough of the food for everyone.

She would beg her husband to let her children alone in the woods and then abandon them. Her reasoning was that once they had been there, they wouldn't be able to return home. She believed that somewhere, someone could come across them, and give them a decent home.

When Hansel was listening to his parents talk about this in the evening and thought of putting together an idea to make sure that it was always possible to return home He did this by putting pebbles in the pocket of his. If he was in the woods and was in the forest, he would walk couple of steps, and then drop pebbles.

After he had been removed from the forest, he was able to return home via the pebbles. He as well as his sister remained in the forest. However, his step-mother was unhappy and wanted to make sure they would stay within the woods. The house was filled with sadness His father made a decision that he'd let his kids go to woods. Hansel made the trail of crumbs instead of pebbles, and birds devoured them. His sister and he were unable to get to home.

They walked through the woods until they came to an odd house that was comprised of biscuits and chocolate. They started eating in the home because they were hungry, and then the door was opened and they saw an elderly woman. They were invited in and she began to feed them to make them fatter. She would touch their fingers. She could tell if they were becoming more fatter. Then, when they were at the right size, she attempted to cook them and transform into food.

They were locked in the house and were contemplating the possibility of death. To keep themselves safe they forced her into the fire. she was smoldering to on the ground. Then, they walked around the house and collected the most gold they could. They then headed into the forest with a goal to return home.
As they walked back to their homes they saw their father, who was crying since he lost his family after his wife's death. They rushed up to him and embraced him and made promises to him that he would never leave them. He was delighted to hear that. They gave him the gold and said that they would never be ever again poor. Thus they were happy for ever after as an entire family.

This tale provides a lot of information about the lives of people living at the time. There was a lot of poverty and everything that looked like a way towards escaping it was taken. There was a sense of insatiableness and a desire to look after self, with no regard for the needs of others. While this might seem cruel however, from the other perspective it could have just been just a matter of survival.

Also, there was a huge number of deaths as is evident by the woodcutter who lost his wife. While the cause of the deaths isn't known but it is likely that they died due to sudden illness. It was not easy and it was difficult to live there were incidents of murder and theft. There were also stories of those who survived and who used their skills to survive in an ever-changing world. In this whole book, you will find people you've met that made the choice to live their lives with courage and, in some instances they were able to demonstrate affection even during the toughest of times. The middle ages witnessed that the beginning of genius and reason, of perseverance and of courage. Whoever was able to make it through it was awe-inspiring.

Chapter 5: Calligraphy In The World

Beautiful certificates as well as timeless documents and manuscripts that make a lasting impression are often distinguished because of the artistic writing. The artful lettering is referred to by the Greek word "calligraphy. It literally means "beautiful lettering". Calligraphy is handwriting that's elegant and beautiful. Nowadays, calligraphy is an art form that is stunning and expressive.

Calligraphy is used in many writing systems around the world , in a variety of scripts. When you read the calligraphy script in English it shows innovative ways to utilize the letters of the Latin alphabet. The most popular scripts around the world are East Asian, which have Chinese, Japanese and Korean scripts to give examples, Arabic scripts as well as Indic and Cyrillic scripts. This section will provide you with the foundation of these systems as well as how to utilize them to create your own style of typography.

Writing in Chinese

The only thing that writing systems that originate from East Asia have in common is the usage of characters and symbols. They do not have an alphabet that you encounter in Latin scripts. They make characters by using different strokes that give the meaning of their words,

The scripts of the past, especially, considered writing as a technique and an art form, and the method in which scripts were written conveyed more than just the message. They also expressed the feelings of the calligrapher. Every letter in Chinese writing is words that have one syllable or of the syllables within the larger word. This is known as logo-syllabic. Each character is unique and, consequently, should you be capable of writing every word of this writing system, you would have to memorize 4000 characters.

If writing Chinese the calligrapher employs strokes that in the past were drawn using an ink brush. Modern writing uses strokes. orders have been developed to make it easier to recall more characters and facilitates faster writing. To write the strokes, you need to move your fingers in specific directions, for example, from top to bottom. Also, you must move your hand horizontally prior to vertical or left to right, and the list goes on. To master these skills, you will need to acquire each stroke separately and after that, you'll be able to connect the strokes together when needed to make characters.

Calligraphers who write in Chinese will notice that it is possible to write horizontally as well as vertically. If writing vertically, the characters should be written in a vertical order from bottom to top and when writing horizontally they are written from the left to right. The symbol can also be written from the left to right.

Different scripts

The scripts you employ for writing in calligraphic scripts alter with time. In the Chinese instance, the scripts have evolved over time and have evolved from having elements which were straight and precise, to cursive scripts that are simpler to understand. This is why it's sometimes difficult to read documents written centuries ago. Certain scripts have become heavier because they've grown in size. The symbols in the script were separate earlier, nowadays they are joined and this indicates it is removed from the paper less frequently.

In official papers, you can use the normal script, where each line is written extreme attention to ensure there is a distinct symbol within the characters. When compared with that of the Latin alphabet, this will be similar to capital letters.

Writing in Arabic

Arabic calligraphy is beautiful and gorgeous, and just like Chinese there are a myriad of styles and techniques. Arabic is a script that originates from the ancient Aramaic script. There are 28 letters, which have lines as well as dots.

A calligrapher might be able to write in Arabic difficult as the forms of the letters vary based on the position they are in within a word. It is essential to keep an appropriate proportion in Arabic script. From the highest point that the Alif (the initial letter in the alphabet) it is possible to identify a specific calligrapher.

Every word is written if it were designed to fit into the imaginary circle. Therefore, when you are learning you write Arabic it is important keep this in mind when writing your letters. Arabic script has the use of angular writing, cursive writing hanging letters, and even script specifically made to be used by royalty.

The text is written bidirectional fashion that is, the text can move in a left-to-right direction however, it is mostly written from left to right. The direction that the letters' movement will occur will influence the way the calligrapher draws them. This kind of writing requires gentle pressure.

In the Latin Alphabet

The current Latin alphabet is utilized in the majority of writing across the world, particularly in European languages. It is comprised of 26 letters, however there are variations that contain diacritics too that extend the alphabet substantially. There is even the possibility to expand the Latin alphabet by forming the ligatures (the connecting of letters) or by clustering letters. In writing calligraphy, these modifications to the alphabet can influence the way in which the calligraphy technique is employed to write the words.

The Latin alphabet contains the letters in uppercase as well as lowercase. They can be written as a line that moves from left to right. There are many fonts that work using that Latin alphabet, meaning the text could be square, cursive or rounded, or even mixed cases. Calligraphy utilizing an Latin alphabet is commonly used in documents to give it an attractive appearance.

There are numerous other writing styles from around the globe. These influence the ways people write beautiful writing material. The three systems discussed within this section are among the most frequently used across the globe. For a calligrapher, being conscious of various writing techniques will help you learn to use different methods to ensure that the text you write can convey the message you want to convey.

Calligraphy goes beyond writing. It's a way to express feelings , and it brings life to words. This in mind, you are now able to start making and perfecting your art. The next chapter will let know how to do in order to start.

Chapter 6: Putting The Fundamentals Together

For you to begin your journey towards learning calligraphy you'll need a variety of things available. When you were younger, you'd have used a brush, a pot of black ink , and some parchment to use. Nowadays, calligraphy is more sophisticated, and the tools that you can employ are been developed.

The essential tools that you will require include an eraser and pencil. These tools will assist you with your practice as well as the basic symbols. Then, you will need paper that you can utilize as a practice sheet. In order to help you become more precise the paper must be lined.

The next essential thing you require is the pen holder. It is the portion of the pen that you carry in your palm. It will come with a section of it that allows you to swap the tips of your pen.

Tips

Calligraphy today is a process that requires using a pencil to create writing on paper. There are a myriad of different scripts that you could create, and since each script needs a specific techniques and pressure You will require various pen techniques.

The tip itself is extremely complex, and is comprised of seven components. Beginning at the bottom is the base. It will be followed by the body. There is a vent hole. Above this there is the shoulder. There is a tiny line that is known as the slit. It runs up to the point of the compound, or point. In the slit there are tines.

Chiseled or Flat-Tipped Nibs

These kinds of nibs are flat and wide They are ideal for those who want to begin calligraphy. You can draw different letters and also make various strokes. They come in a variety of widths on the tip since it's the tip of the nib that's consistently large. The ideal nib to choose is one with an 8-inch width. or one-quarter inch. If you write with an upward stroke, it will appear wide. If you write using an upward stroke the letter will be thinner. The nibs that are thinner are better at holding ink and consequently, they're more frequently dipped than pointed nibs. They are not elastic.

Poster Nib

If the nib that has a flat tipped tip were to have a larger brother, this is it. The nibs are big and broad and can be used to write using large type. Due to their size they have an ink reservoir which is integrated and the touch of the tip is soft instead of sharp.

Pointed Nibs

They are extremely popular with contemporary calligraphers because they are simpler to use as well as flexible enough for you to test different scripts. As with the flat-tipped nibs, these come in a variety of sizes, so you can choose which you feel more comfortable using. The sizes are divided in four key categories. They include extremely fine, that is identified by the letters EF Fine with F, medium with the letters M, and B to indicate Broad. These nibs are famous as being flexible which can be useful for making broad strokes.

Drawing Nibs

They are the tiniest you can find and are point-like in their design. They are great for drawing precise lines. When used for writing letters, they are prone to catch on paper easily and require constant cleaned. This is why they're better suited for drawings or hatchings.

Nib Holder

Your nibs or tips must be placed in the nib holder to be used. The nib holder you pick will be constructed out of one of two materials: plastic or wood. For those who are just beginning it is recommended to pick a nib holder which is straight. If you examine the part where you plan to place the nib in there, you'll notice the presence of a metal rings, and inside contains prongs like those found on the screw head. When you insert the nib into place it is important to ensure that it fits in from the base and is placed between the prongs on the inside and the ring made of metal. The nib should not be placed between the prongs of the inner one. It must be firmly fitted to allow you to write clearly.

Ink

Most calligraphy is written using black ink. In the past, people used to make their own ink by made from natural substances and water. Today, you can buy ink that is premixed and ready to use. The best ink for you to begin with is known as India ink.

In addition to the ink, you'll need an incredibly small container of water. It is the perfect place to dip your tip into at times, since your tip may get clogged.

Paper

The type of paper you select for calligraphy is essential in order to achieve a clear and precise results. The past was when bamboo-based parchment and reeds was the preferred choice to write on. Since calligraphy has evolved from nibs to brushes as tools for writing smooth, smooth papers are the ideal for calligraphy. The paper that's rough, or even textured can create particles inside the nib that could cause mistakes while writing.

The paper should be a little transparent. It is vital to ensure that it doesn't leak. This is why normal printing papers are not suitable because the ink could be splattered and writing would become unclear. Paper for watercolor painting is perfect because of its capacity to absorb ink and paint quickly.

Guide Sheet

If you're just beginning in calligraphy, you'll need to try your best to draw straight lines every time. If your paper is non-lined, this might be difficult. This is why you must have a guide sheet. The guide sheet is composed of dark lines. Then, you should put your transparent paper over your guide sheet. To ensure that your guide sheet isn't moving it, secure it to the table you're using with tape. This will allow you to write straight without making any marks that are obvious on the paper.

Cleaning

To ensure that you get the best results from your nib it is necessary to regularly clean it, particularly because particles may get stuck within the slit of the nib. To do this make sure you make use of water and wipe down the nib using a soft cloth and clean. It is important to remember that before using it for the first time, it needs to be cleaned with the softest cloth and rubbing alcohol. This is due to the fact that when they are made in the first place, they are coated with a chemical residue , so they are shielded from corrosion. If you don't wash this off when you writing, the oil in the chemical residue could impact how well you write your writing.

Brushing with an Brush

You might decide that you would rather stick to traditional and study the art of calligraphy using brushes instead of nibs and tips commonly used nowadays. It is easy to achieve this by using the brush pen along with some paper. Brush pen can bring the traditional to the contemporary because it's an instrument that doesn't run out of ink quickly and prevents frequent dips. It is also referred to as a marker, but one of the features that makes it ideal to be used for writing is the flexible tip. The tip allows you to alter the way in which you write on paper by applying pressure. It is likely that brush pens can be found in a variety of sizes to allow for greater flexibility.

Finding what you require to calligraph isn't difficult because the majority of art supply stores along with those that sell stationery will stock these products.

Chapter 7: Learn Stokes And Curves And Developing Your Technique

With the equipment you've got, you're able to start to build your skills as calligraphers. The first step to learn is how to utilize your tools. This is how you begin.

The Dip

The first step is of learning how to use your method. You should have your pencil along with a paper and a pot of ink ready. Be sure that your pen is equipped with an eight-inch diameter tip. While holding your pen with a firm grip and dipping the tip into the ink slowly until the ink has reached a level approximately 3/4 up the tip.

The Hold

The way you hold your pen is vital in order to prevent shaking, which can interfere with the ability of writing smooth. Your grip should be soft but solid. If you grip you pen in a tight way, the hands is likely to get fatigued quicker and result in shaking.

The First Letter

The process of writing your very first word should be a pleasant experience. Start by placing your pens tips down on your paper. This will stop you from scratching your paper because the sides of your pen tips will likely be sharp. Before writing your letter, it is important to practice your strokes. On your sheet, sketch out a few lines, making sure that you have straight lines and curved ones. When you've done this and you'll begin to realize how much ink you'll need to write with, and also how to determine what amount of color you need to put on the tip. You'll get a sense of writing. By using an alphabet called the Latin Alphabet, you can create your very first alphabet. Now you don't need to think about the typeface you're using, just create the word.

For instance, if write in the alphabet A make a note of how you are using your pen tip while writing. What direction is your hand moving? Are all of your lines straight? Or did you have curves? Was there a succession of lines? Or was this just one rapid move? Do you see a slant within the word or does it appear straight? Answering these questions will provide an understanding of your basic technique.

The Downward Stroke

In calligraphy, the primary stroke you will use is an upward stroke. To become familiar with this stroke, do as many times as you can before writing an initial letter. On paper that is lined, you can use the pen tip to draw an outline from the top to the bottom. The point where your pen is in contact with paper and then when it stops making contact you'll notice there's a small foot inside the line. It's normal. Additionally, if your natural line has a slant it is normal. Its direction will be contingent on whether you're right or left handed. If you are left-handed, the slant will shift towards the left, and the same applies if you happen to be right-handed. While you work you will see that after just a few lines down strokes, your downward strokes be much improved.

Certain letters require both the downward and upward stroke. When making these writings, you must apply pressure to your nibs on the downward strokes and make sure that you do not apply pressure to those upward strokes. This implies that the upward strokes appear thinner as compared to the lower strokes when you write.

The most dominant stroke you use to write is horizontal downwards stroke. From that stroke, you will shift to a new direction. this is called branching. It's usually an arc diagonal stroke. You might want to think about writing capital letters A. After you have completed the downward stroke vertically it is necessary to make a new stroke.

Other Strokes

There are many different strokes that you could utilize in calligraphy in addition to the primary downward stroke. There are also pull and push strokes. They are employed to cross letters such as the lower and upper cases of T, and F. F. This bar used to cross is smaller than the downward vertical stroke which makes up the remainder of the letters.

Additionally, there are horizontal strokes that can be located at the bottom and the top of alphabets.

The entrance stroke can be used for all characters of the alphabet, and it's an upward stroke that is thin. It is able to start or finish a letter as well as begin the letter halfway. A different stroke commonly utilized prior to the opening stroke would be the stroke called an underturn. It's shaped like an U. It starts with a downward stroke which is very thick, but then it changes into a thin stroke and then finally, it is it's entrance stroke. It is commonly used in conjunction with vowels such as I and u, as well as with the letters d as well as t and w. The letters all use the stroke with lowercase.

Overturn is the term used to describe a turn of the stroke that is underturn. The U shape appears upside down. For the first time you write letters using this shape, you'll have hairline strokes that begin at the base. As it curves back the stroke will shift into a thick downward stroke. The key to this is about the pressure you employ in writing.

The Curve

It is the downward stroke that's the primary stroke you employ when writing calligraphy. Another option to the downward stroke is the curve. Consider that letter C in the current Latin alphabet. It is the best illustration of what a curve ought to appear like. Thus, using lined paper, you can draw your curve spaces between lines. Your curve will be moving towards the left and then you'll feel a soft dislodging of the pen off the paper at the final point of your curve. Contrary to the downward stroke, in which your letter will have one foot at the top the curve shouldn't appear to have this. It should appear smooth. To improve your writing skills Practice and then try to create a complete line that has a lot of curves.

The downward stroke and curve are essential to keep in mind when writing calligraphy since you'll notice that nearly all letters are built on these two letters. After you've practiced using the flat tip then you can try using them on a variety of tips. This will give you a greater understanding of how to test different calligraphic techniques.

It is crucial to apply just enough ink onto your tip. If it's too small and your ink is not enough, it will dry quickly while you write and you'll end up with scratchy and unattractive lines on the paper. Additionally, you might not be able finish the letters correctly, so your calligraphy may lack the luster and flow. If, on the other hand you've got excessive to write with ink it will result in the ink dripping onto the paper in a flurry that will result in streaks that can make your calligraphy look messy.

Writing, you must to be aware of the basics of the art of writing, and that's callingigraphy requires the use of more than your wrist and fingers. Be sure to have enough space as you'll also have to move your arms and even your shoulders to create gorgeous letters. If you're right handed, ensure that ink is on the right side of your paper because this will allow you to avoid spills of ink. Similar principles apply to left handed people as well.

To develop your skills and become a proficient calligrapher, it is essential to do as much practice as you can. The more you practice the more, you'll be amazed by the results you can accomplish.

Chapter 8: Lettering

You're now ready to try a variety of styles and fonts so that you can start creating beautiful calligraphy. Before you start you must be aware of the various ways in which letters within a word are deferred and the rope these letters draw.

Capital Letters

They are letters that are uppercase. They are typically used at starting sentences, phrases, or for the start of names. They tend to be more hefty than other letters because they are written using a downward stroke.

Lowercase letters

They are also known as small letters, and constitute the majority of the words they appear in.

Cap Height

When writing capital letters, you could be writing a letter that is flat, like either N or I, or a letter that is rounded, such as C or Q, or one that is pointed like the letters A and X. The height of the cap corresponds to the letter's height in uppercase. It is directly related to letters that are flat.

X-Height

The following three lines that must be taken into consideration when determining the x-height. The first line is the baseline (which is discussed later in the chapter) There is also the waistline, and finally the height of the cap. When writing lowercase letters you determine its height by x. This is the area of lowercase letters that does not have ascenders or descenders. The lowercase body of the letter is located on the line between waistline and baseline, and the distance between the two lines is known as the height of the x.

Baseline

The base is the beginning the writing you write, and it will guide your letters and assure that you're writing stunning. This is that all your letters are allowed to rest and ensure that your writing stays clean and well-organized.

Hairline

A hairline is a thin line that you see in a letter. To draw or write hairlines, you'll have to draw using the nib's tip however, you should not apply any pressure to the paper when doing this. The nib should simply move across on top. Every upward stroke you make will be considered as hairlines. It is important to remember that hairlines can be drawn in any direction you prefer.

Waistline

Above the line, you'll notice the waistline. The line changes in its height according to the height of the letter that is being written. Lowercase letters have their bodies are placed between that line at the base. If you can cover the ascenders and descenders, you'll be able to determine the lowercase letters that can be found within the designated space.

Ascender

When writing lowercase letters you'll notice your letters located within two lines. This is the baseline line and waistline. Some letters are taller and extend beyond the waistline up to that of the height cap. The portion of the letter which rises over the waistline can be known by the term "ascender. It is seen in a variety of lowercase letters that include the letters h and l.

Descender

Descenders can also be referred to as lowercase letters. They are located between the baseline and above what's known as beard lines. This implies that there is one part in the letters that's more that the other, and it is usually known as the tail. It is commonly found in letters like the letters p or y.

Crossbar

There is a variety of letters that are both lowercase and uppercase with a crossbar as they are writing. In lowercase, one of the most popular examples is the letter T. It is essential to keep in mind when writing on this letter, you'll have to lift your hands above the paper to write two strokes. Similar is the case for the capital letter H.

Flourish

This adds a visual element to your writing . typically occurs in the last part of sentences or in the place where it is followed by a descenter or tail. It is also employed to create a beautiful look to the word's beginning. The joy of living can raise a word's significance.

When you write calligraphy, it is important to ensure that the letters are correctly proportional. Therefore when a word requires some amount of downward strokes within the letters, try to ensure that all downward strokes are identical. This is achievable when you can manage your nib. The pressure you put on your fingers must be low enough that it doesn't alter the aesthetics in the written word. Additionally, applying excessive force on your nib, which is very sensitive could cause damage to it.

The baseline you choose to use should be as stable as you can Otherwise, you'll end in writing that's not even, transforming beautiful writing into something ugly and even difficult to comprehend.

The height of the cap aswell as the x-height need to be uniform. This means that capital letters must be the same size and you should not emphasize only one letter while allowing the other letters with a smaller size.

With ascenders and descenters the importance of height is increased. A guide sheet can help maintain these in check. The height of the ascender should not be higher than the height of a capital letter and the lower height should be just lower than the line that is writing so that it's not too low.

Also, the white spaces between words are as crucial just as words They should be at least two letters in length between words, in order that a connection is made without causing overcrowding.

In order to improve your abilities and techniques in lettering, it is important be able to examine every element of writing a letter as an individual. This means that the elements are not able to be memorized as a whole.

They must be learned and practiced in their own way.

Chapter 9: Overcoming Calligraphy Challenges

As you grow into a prolific calligrapher, and carry on in your journey you'll notice that there are some issues that you will have to solve and overcome. This chapter provides suggestions to help you achieve a seamless writing experience each time.

Start Your Day Comfortably

This is the most important one because it's the one that's most crucial and yet the most neglected. To be able to create beautiful calligraphy, you have to be in a positive mindset, and you need to be relaxed. Thus, you must first clear your thoughts to allow you to concentrate on the task in present. Find the chair that is comfortable and allows you to sit up straight. It is important to maintain a healthy posture by making sure your back is in a straight line and your feet flat on the floor. Make sure that the desk you're working at is free of clutter and you only have the tools you'll require.

Ink isn't flowing

It is quite frustrating trying to write the words on paper, only to find that your ink isn't flowing. Most likely, the reason it happens is due to the way that you hold your nib and pen. It is important to be holding it at a 45 degree angle to achieve the best outcomes.

This could also happen in the event that you are using an entirely new or different nib, and using ink that you have never used before. To make sure that the ink flows after you've put the nib in it, you need to take the end of the nib, and then quickly dip it into water. Be sure to dip only towards the edge of the nib. The ink flows more fluidly.

Snagging Pen

There are occasions when you'll notice your pen is snagging on paper since the nib is held to the paper's fibers. The ink will begin to splash onto the paper which can affect the aesthetic appearance of your writing. To stop this from occurring, you have to be aware of the pressure you place on your nib while writing. When you write with upstrokes, make sure that the pressure you apply is light. Don't force the nib too far on the sheet of paper.

Clogging Ink

The ink that you use can block the flow for various reasons. The most common reason is that it begins to dry out after having it open over a long period of time, which makes it thick enough to be able to slide off the nib easily. When this occurs, grab just a few drop of water, and add them to the ink to thin it out. Continue to practice writing letters until you're proficient at writing smoothly. Incorporate a small amount water at a moment to continue thinning the ink If necessary.

The ink may also build in your nib. This happens if the nib is dirty or there are numerous fibers stuck near the edge. To get rid of this problem take care to clean the nib cleaning it in water, then wipe it dry with the soft, clean cloth.

Thin Ink

In your desire to alter the consistency of your ink you might have created it too thin instead of thick. You can make it thicker with the addition of some Arabic. Make sure you add only the right amount. It is important to remember the fact that this will thicken as time.

How do you thicken the ink

Pour ink into a different container and do not put the ink back into the original ink jar, since if you make mistakes by pouring on too much, you'll be wasting a lot ink.

- Grab your ink thickener and add several drops at a moment into the separate container.

The next step is trial and error. Once you have succeeded in mixing in the thickener ink, you'll have to test the mixture using a different piece paper to check whether the ink has stopped bleeding (see bleeding explanation below) If you've added too much ink and it sticks to the nib and not write smooth.

It is essential to test the thickener in your ink alongside your ink to determine whether they're compatible. often they do not mix well and you may use up many gallons of ink because it's not usable.

It is true that top quality products will work better so you should to invest in them if are able.

The Letters You Need to Write

Calligraphy is a craft and an art, which means that when you get your nib and pen for writing, you have to be committed to perfecting the art and doing it well. It can only be done through consistent practice and regular. Spending at least 20 minutes every day to practice strokes as well as curves and letters can help you improve your skills when using the pen, as well as when creating outcomes that look appealing.

The method you use to are practicing is equally important when you're interested in seeing results. Learn to practice the curves and strokes in various ways. With different pens, you can find out how you can make thick strokes as well as broad strokes. While doing this, you should perfect the angle you use to place your nib to the paper. To improve your technique you should also practice drawing circles and shapes on the paper. This will assist you in using your pen correctly when writing.

Making the incorrect Paper

There's paper that's not suitable for calligraphy and the more you try to work with it the more frustrated will be as you do never see the results you want. Be sure to avoid drawing on printer paper or drawing, since they will bleed and alter the appearance of your writing. Additionally, craft and recycled papers have excessive texture and fiber that will alter the nib as well as the slit. The rough watercolor paper is not the best for calligraphy.

Avoiding Mistakes

There are bound to be mistakes when working with calligraphy, but you can prevent them by using this method. Always keep a piece of paper in your hand to allow you to check the flow of your ink before you begin writing. This way, you'll be able determine whether your ink has clogged up or flowing too slow , or if the paper is bleeding. It is then possible to check that your ink is in the right consistency before starting to correct. This will prevent you from making a mistake that can make you restart.

The process of achieving Perfection

With all the information you are aware of about calligraphy it is tempting to hurry out, grab your nibs and ink , and start. It's more beneficial to practice first with an array of more basic materials. Start your journey using a eraser and pencil, then purchase a drawing or writing pad as well as a ruler. Be aware of how you can make your letters to be perfectly aligned and also the format you can choose to your calligraphy. This will aid you in creating your letters to are uniform.

Bleeding Ink

In some instances, you could encounter what's called "ink bleeding" or "feathering'. It could appear as if that water has fallen on the ink, causing it to spread , ruining your work. There are many reasons this might be happening: the paper could be damp and the paper may be of poor quality as well as the ink used could have a thin consistency. There's nothing you can do when the paper you've used has been affected by moisture but unfortunately. It is necessary to replace the paper and begin again in the event that the work you've completed is not usable. However, there is a way you can do if the ink isn't thick enough.

When something goes wrong when you work on your calligraphy, make sure you do not get caught out. Making mistakes is an essential element of the process since it helps you improve your technique overall.

Chapter 10: The History Of Writing

How often do you visit the library? The world of the internet is what it is today , and information available in a plethora of ways and accessible, it is odd to think we would visit the library for the information we required. "Google it" was not even a thought and you'd never be able to put off your University homework until the late night because you'd require the source of the information before you go to the library to refer to it in a proper manner. If you've visited the library in recent times take a look back at the number of books available and then realize that at one time, they all were written in hand.

Before the invention of printing, libraries existed. There were fewer libraries and you needed to have a degree to access them, however they were there and the books available required handwriting. Novels, encyclopedias and even works of non-fiction were created by pen and ink. The first editions of the most famous books like The Old as well as the New Testament or Greek and Latin texts were all written in hand. The origins of writing could be traced as far back as Ancient Egypt. The use of hieroglyphics also known as picture writing was created on clay tablet, walls, and sculptures.

Prior to Pen, Ink and Parchment

What was the first thing that paper did before? This isn't a traditional tale about what preceded the chicken or the egg? Writing was invented prior to paper, or perhaps the pencil and the ink. There are many theories about the origins of writing. Christians think they believe that the Bible was discovered written on stone, and later rewritten on parchment. Was that the way it began? It is believed that writing on stones was the first type of penmanship. It was then writing on bark ripped from trees. If you could imagine the hassle of having to write important letters by stone, it would create an administrative nightmare, and the demand for writing wouldn't have risen to the level that it did.

The process of cutting into the stone to write was laborious and required endurance and perseverance. Academics would probably not have carved into the stone by themselves however, they would have had students or colleagues each record their observations. At the time of writing into stone, it was not employed to record notes or thoughts. It would be difficult and would take a lot of time

They needed something that was lighter and easy to use. Thus came the need for the bark of trees as well as wax tablets.

There is evidence in the past that the introduction of wax tablets and bark as "paper"; writing was used less frequently. Pens were used to write on bark. This created additional problems due to the ink would leak into the wood, rendering it virtually unreadable. When writing important historical documents the method was not acceptable. The students of the future would never have been in a position to read the texts and their knowledge wouldn't have been passed to the next generation. The wax tablets allowed for better writing, and the Romans employed a stylus made of metal to scratch out letters. This was extremely slow and was used to create more important historical pieces instead of day-to-day correspondence.

Writing Styles

In the early days the font was created by New Roman cursive. It wasn't the most elegant type of font since it was not very elegant and was hard to read. Writing was so rare and a rare thing, it was logical to write poorly at the moment that required it. They also recognized that since the content was considered to be of high value such as writing in the Bible or other ancient texts There had to be the right style for it to be in line with. The style of uncial was used and the writing was done with an enormous straight-cut edge pen, which created words that were incredibly big and took up a lot of space. Naturally, they thought that this was perfect due to the content which is being discussed. The Church would teach monks of Latin in writing and reading. The monks who were artistic would make replicas of the Bible.

A different style that was used in lesser-known works was known as Insular Minuscule, which is a stylized and sharp writing style. In the late 19th century, writing was used more frequently. It was becoming more popular to keep more records and used the medium in everyday communication rather than only for recording holy artifacts and crucial writings from the past. This type of writing was also employed throughout the 9th Century as a bookhand.

The world began to change under the period of the reign of Emperor Charlemagne in the 9th century. He was referred to for his role as

Charles the Great. He was responsible for unifying the vast majority of Europe and for laying the groundwork for the modern France in addition to Germany. In his 13-year rule as the emperor and emperor, he was known as being on constantly on the move and in the midst of a rush. While he was at it, he also enjoyed reading books and frequently presented them as gifts to nobles. Even though he was unable to write, he thought it was necessary to simplify ways of writing to make them more easy to understand. He wanted to write quickly and easily. Remember that the words were much larger due to the 'pen which was in use and filled up more space than they do to be able to do today. He argued for a more user-friendly font should be developed so that books could be smaller, and the user more at ease. The style of writing was referred to as Caroline Minuscale and it was also used for writing the Bible in the abbey of St Martin in France, an approach to writing that swiftly spread to England and the United Kingdom as well.

As time went by the forward-slanting letterforms were more sturdy and attractive. With more ascenders, and shorter descenders, this style of writing was utilized to create the Ramsey Psalter. The foundational hand was the style of writing spotted as such by Edward Johnston who is considered the founder of calligraphy in the beginning of the 20th Century. As we moved forward to the 11th century, the letters that were rounded became smaller as words were squeezed into smaller space. The style that was compressed was referred to as English Caroline Minuscale Compressed.

Full Gothic writing was developed during the latter half of the 12th century, and is the style that appears in a variety of famous novels. It is known for its weighty as well as rigid look, Gothic Black Letter saw the majority of letters that were rounded turn straight. This made it difficult to read and was not quite as elegant as the previous writing styles, and a lot of people were not a fan of this type of writing. At the time of writing it was used to create documents, letters and charters. It was more common by people today than it was at the time of the 9th century, when only a handful of people knew the art of writing. The majority of people began using it in their daily and private lives in their private lives and it became a more widespread knowledge than it was prior to.

The Origin of Italic

The Humanists in Italy during the Renaissance weren't happy in The Gothic Black Letter and tried to create a more human appearance writing style. They resisted the rigidity and rigidity that was characteristic of Gothic designs and looked to the past to find sources of inspiration. When they looked back to Charlemagne They believed they could see that Caroline Minuscale was more fitting to the Renaissance period, when things were changing and more artistic and creative. They didn't fully emulate it, however they took elements from it, and then transformed Caroline Minuscale to what they called Humanistic Minuscale. Based on this new style of writing emerged the cursive type that we call Italic. Humanistic Minuscale has often been called the lighter variant of Caroline Minuscale as it appears to be a little more delicate.

Italics was the style of writing that engravers used in the early days and they together with other writers created what's now known as Copperplate writing that utilizes a pointed nib for the writing instrument or "pen". This style of writing is taught at schools and then became popular throughout the world during the 19th century. It was taught to anyone seeking to become clerks within the British Empire.

William Morris

At the close at the end of century William Morris began looking at the styles of writing and techniques used in writing during the medieval era. Morris was a poet, designer novelist, translator and writer from England around 1834. He realized that writing of the medieval period was not accomplished with an instrument with a thin tip, instead, a pen that had a broad edges. In the beginning, it was believed that a pencil with a thin tip could be used for drawing out letters, and it was filled with ink to draw the outline in order to make the words. Morris was a fan of the classics and was awed by medieval manuscripts and made the discovery. This discovery led to the revival of calligraphy.

William Morris did not altogether revitalize the art of calligraphy' Edward Johnston took his initial findings and continued in his research.

Edward Johnston

He is regarded as among the world's most renowned names in the history of calligraphy. Born in 1872 in Uruguay, the Uruguayan and

British artist developed the broad edged tool which is still in use today in calligraphy. He is famous for his creation of the font that was utilized in the famous underground system of London up until the 1980's when it was updated.

Following studying, Edward Johnston was introduced to the head in the Central School of Arts and Crafts William Lethaby. Lethaby directed Johnston to look over medieval manuscripts just as William Morris did. Johnston copied the styles of writing through the creation of the broad edged tool that could produce the similar result. Then, he published Writing & Illuminating & Lettering in 1906. He has been recognized as having revived the penmanship of the modern age.

Chapter 11: Master The Basics

After having learned where calligraphy came from, as well as the various aspects of the tools required and the different writing styles now is the time to get an introduction guide to how to begin. In the next chapter you'll learn about the basics necessary to start and the tools required to master callingigraphy. These items can be purchased in local shops or on the internet according to availability. They are reasonably priced.

Recommendations for Tools and Equipment

- Zebra G Nib. This is a fantastic nib to begin with as it's sturdy and perfect for novices.

Straight Pen or Oblique Pen. It is based on your personal preference. Visit the nearest store to try the pens out before deciding on your own which one you would like to utilize. After you have made your choice make sure you stick to it , as once you are confident, it is difficult to change the pens.

- Tracing Paper.

• Calligraphy Grid. It is available for purchase or downloaded from the social media sites Pinterest as well as Google. It's great to practice and getting your writing as exact as they can be.

- Ink.

A variety of papers.

After you've bought these products It's time to start practicing! For the first step, place the nib into your pen, and then practice holding it until it feels comfortable in your palm. Take off the lid of the inkpot and dip your nib into the inkpot to ensure that the ink hole remains hidden from view. Be sure to gently skim over the sides of your inkpot while you draw the nib from your container to stop you from splashing your ink all over when you begin writing. Even with this method you should lay on some kind of surface to shield the table you're working on. Ink may drip throughout your practice session, since you are beginning to learn, so be cautious.

Let's get started!

Consider the time you first began writing when you were a kid. What did your teacher, or your parents instruct you? The process of learning calligraphy is similar to writing yet again. It's a brand new method of holding your pen. The letters may need to be written in a different way. There are different pressures that are used while writing, and the strokes require time to master.

We'll start from the beginning. Grab your tracing sheet and grid, and arrange them like lines on a paper pad. Be sure to have an old tissue paper or rag nearby to wipe away the ink that has accumulated when you're needed to.

Step One

Begin by using your grid as a guideline and then draw a line along the length of the block on your grid. Be sure to check the result when you apply different pressures. Start by drawing a tiny line, gradually increase the pressure until you are able to observe how thicker your lines will become. it's not that much of pressure to increase size of the lines, so be sure to keep a gentle finger always.

Make sure that the lines are as close as you can. Try to get them to be as close as you can for a full page. It may sound to be too much work, but it is important to know the amount of pressure you apply based on the thickness you'd like to achieve.

Step Two

Create a loopthat looks similar to the letter "I". Be aware of the pressure you apply to the paper based on where you stand with the letter. When you draw, apply very little pressure, and then add a bit of pressure each time the loop is retraced back. As with the lines from Step One, try keep them as evenly distributed as you can and try repeating your loop to make you get the appearance is similar. It's all about repetition! The letters must appear as natural as if you would write the"l "l" using the pencil.

Step Three

Begin with the lowercase alphabet and gradually master each letter individually! Don't be rushed and don't believe that you're cheating by tackling the easiest alphabet first. Download images that are similar to the ones shown below, either on Pinterest and Google. Start with a group regardless of whether it is ascending or descended letters. For an ascending letter, as example, would be"b" for example "b" in which the stroke moves up or up. Keep in mind that you have to master strokes as well as you master the letters. The lowercase ascenders are those letters: b, d F, h as well as l and t. As with the other two steps, fill one page, at least for each letter. Lowercase letters that descend are g, j P, Q and Y and try them following! You'll need to learn, or at the very least feel comfortable with all alphabet letters prior to moving on to capitals or words. After you've mastered both ascending and descending letters of the lowercase alphabet then you can begin to tackle the other letters in the alphabet that are lowercase.

A trick that can be applied to any letter use: apply a minimum of pressure when you climb and increase the pressure when you descend.

Step Four

It's time to begin with words that are short and this essential step because it's the foundations for sentence writing. Begin with two letters at first. Then, you can learn how to connect the words and see whether you can achieve the flow with no lifting the pen. However, don't be afraid to raise your pen at first when you begin; instead, you should get the letters right rather than trying to write whole sentences without raising your pen. Once you've conquered the two letter words, move to three words and move upwards from the beginning. For those who are trying to tackle bigger words s to start with words you're familiar with, similar to your name, and that are easy to remember. The key is to make sure your pen is smooth when you move between letters. This is the time when your pen is required to be the thinnest.

If you require stencils you can find plenty on Google which can be downloaded for free and are a great assistance during this phase.

Important Tips to Calligraphy Prosperity

If you hear scratching when you write It's a sign that the pen is not sitting correctly in your hands . You must adjust your grip

Use less pressure on the upward strokes than on the down strokes

Keep a steady hand when connecting to letters.

The space between words and letters is as important as learning words and letters. Imagine the way your sentence could be like if the spacing were different between your words and letters

Clean your nib before and after use. If the ink is dry and becomes dry, it could cause it to be difficult for you to work with and cause permanent damage

Try practicing on paper scraps prior to beginning the final piece You will soon get into the rhythm of things, and you'll be less likely to make mistakes.

Strategies to be aware of when you practice:

Make sure to keep your downward strokes as close to being parallel to each other as feasible

Maintain the size of the lowercase letters same. Also, make sure that all capital letters are of the same height.

Your tops ascenders as well as the bottoms of your descenders must end in exactly the same point.
- Keep your baseline as consistent as possible
Take note of ensure to ensure that your space between letters and between your words are the same
Calligraphy for Left-Handed Persons
Similar to writing as usual there are a few distinctions when it comes down to writing in calligraphy for left-handed people. Although they're not that different, it's right to have an entire chapter to ensure we're covered for both ends.
Some helpful suggestions:
The same tools are needed; the only thing we need to make is that you buy straight pen rather than an Oblique pen.
Feel at ease to use any type of paper you like, simply turn the chosen paper by 20 degrees to create a more relaxing environment
Consider the way you hold your pen. Whether your wrist bends , or your hand is curled around the pen. This can affect the way you write and the way you write, once you're at ease with your pen, it will be much easier for you.

- Repetition every letter, as described in the previous chapter

Learn a New Lettering Style
After you've learned the fundamental calligraphy style, there's many more styles to learn and learn to master. Do not be afraid to experiment with different things and download the latest designs that you can share with fellow calligraphy enthusiasts. Practice the new style for at least an hour following your introduction to it. This will allow you to keep the style and get used to your new style of writing or the numbers. Here is an example of the lettering style that is different from that you have learned previously Miniscules, and Numerals:

Chapter 12: Being Creative With Different Mediums Writing On Wood

Calligraphy is infinite because there are numerous ways to use this ability! One of the most appealing aspects about it is that you are able to use different materials to create different decorative items. One of the most popular options in interior design, or for special occasions like weddings is writing on wood. It's not as easy to write on a wood surface. It requires practice , and a few other tools that are affordable enough to buy. It's not as simple as it may seem, but here are some tools that can help you get started:

- Your wooden surface. It is possible to cut it to the size you want, or give it a an aged look and rough cut from wood. Plywood can also be used depending on the style you're looking for Sanding down the surface will help you use. You can also purchase pieces already cut at a craft shop which can cut down on work time and make it little bit easier.

-- Wood Stain. It is available at craft stores, or in your local hardware store

Gloves, latex or any other

A mixing device to mix your paint is something you can find in your home

Sand paper or use an electronic power sander. It's all about your level of confidence and it's more than feasible to work manually, however, it is a good idea to be confident about the equipment, it's an effective time-saver

A clean piece of fabric, soft comfortable is the best choice

Painters tape. It can be bought in the store for hardware

A paint pen of the color of your choice

Step One

It is necessary to prepare the wood prior to being able to utilize it. The cut you've chosen and the style you are planning to create, you can sand the areas you'll use to write. This will make writing more comfortable and smoother for display purposes. If you've chosen an unfinished cut of wood, only sand the area you'll write on and keep the rest of the wood unfinished.

Step Two

The wood will be stained and you'll require your latex gloves to complete this process. Take your stain off carefully with gloves on and mix it with your paint mixing equipment. After the ingredients are mixed, grab your clean cloth and dip it in the stain. Be cautious when taking it out. Be sure to cover your work space as the stain may drip when it moves between your wood and container. If you're painting both wood sides at the same time, begin with the back portion Stain it by wiping the fabric with stain evenly across the wood surface. After you are satisfied, let the wood to air dry before flipping it over and applying the front. One coat is all you need however you are able to apply additional coats until you achieve the color you're looking for. The drying process can take up to several days, dependent on the degree of dryness that the timber is. We strongly recommend allowing drying time for the timber for at minimum for a night. If the stain on the wood isn't completely dry it could negatively affect the final result as the paint will leak into the wood, giving an unfinished look instead of clear strokes. Give yourself a full day for preparation, and then another day to complete the writing because you'll need the wood to dry.

Tips: To determine whether your wood is dry, simply tap on the service, and ensure that it's not sticky. If you feel a bit sticky is a sign that the wood needs more time.

Step Three

This is the time to have fun. You can mark the area you want for your text to be written using paint tape. It is possible to use the tape as a ruler. Draw the line above your temporary line, then finish your descenders after you have removed the tape. It is a good idea to design or measure your board in a way that it's even and has enough room to accommodate your designs. Make sure that your spacing is not consistent between words or letters, your design will not look excellent. The most important aspect of calligraphy is the ability to evenly spread your words and letters for the final appearance correct. Determine the spacing, and if you're an absolute beginner, draw your message using pencil initially. You are able to erase it easily when everything is dry.

Step Four

Use your paint pen to begin slow. In order to make it appear like calligraphy, be careful with the pressure and ensure you don't apply a great deal of pressure at the beginnings or ends of any letter. This puts the danger of creating a look dirty by applying an blot-like effect on the letter's end. It is important practise using the pen since the nib could be different from what you're accustomed to. Make sure you tilt the pen's tip to create the desired effect of calligraphy. As discussed in Chapter 7 Practice is the key to perfecting your skills and it's normal to practice lettering several times before using the first pen. The majority of paint pens don't have the same thickness as regular nibs, so you'll be required to outline your writing and then fill the letters in later when you are ready. When you fill them in that you do not apply too much pressure , or the paint will run through the lines that you have drawn and give your words a feathered appearance. When drawing the outline, it is possible to begin by writing it out using only a single line, gradually 'thickening the line by drawing it into it with a second stroke.

Step Five

Make sure you clean up the mess. Make sure there is no trace left behind by your painters tape . Also, make sure that you've erased all of your pencil marks. Move a few steps away from the work area and make sure that the coloring is especially evident on the areas you colored parts of the alphabet.

Chapter 13: "The One Who Sleeps Never"

Justinian is the name given to the child of founders of the Dynasty Justin, Sabbatius, renamed "Justin I. At an early stage of life, Justinian was mentored for his role as the next Emperor.

Justinian I was a worthy recipient of the slogan

"The The Emperor who Never Sleeps"
because he devoted the majority of his time working for his people. Justinian reigned from Constantinople (currently Istanbul). Historiography considers Justinian I as an experienced legislator with wisdom and compassion. He was a leader of his time due to the fact that he rescued what was important from the rubble from the Ancient Roman Empire. Due to his many accomplishments for the advancement of mankind He was also referred to as "Justinian the great."

While many barbarians threatened the Eastern frontiers, Justinian was an educated man. He was not well-trained in military abilities, and he relied on his generals Belisarius as well as Hermogenes to lead his Byzantine army.

The Corpus Juris Civilis

W
without laws that require respect, civilizations are at risk of the possibility of collapse. Thus, Justinian developed a code of law. His Corpus (also known as the "Body of Civil Law" was a reversal of the primary idea:

"Justice is the unending and constant desire to give everyone the respect he deserves. Law's principals are: to be honest and to not hurt anyone and to pay every man the justice he deserves."

Justinian's Hidden Agenda

Justinian was looking to expand the boundaries within the Eastern Empire - that of Iberia (today's country of Turkey). Iberia was a region which was located just East of his borders. It was an almond-shaped area which included the present-day areas in

Armenia along with that of the North Western area of the Caucasian frontier. Since the region was in his hands, the king also had access to a large portion of the Black Sea.

He also longed for control over his ex-Western Roman Empire, including North Africa including Carthage, the Greek Islands, Sicily and the Island of Sardinia.
First Iberian Campaign 526-532

This country was under the control by the Eastern barbarians, called the Avars and Sassanids. In the strategykon 1 of Maurice an emperor who died later Their forces included:

"...armed with bows, swords and mail and lances. When fighting, most fight with two weapons: lances draped over their shoulders, and bows in their fingers, they employ both when needed. In addition, they are wearing armor on their own and their horses, but those horses used by these famous men are adorned with felt or iron. They pay particular attention to instruction in archery while riding on horses."

The Sassinids were born and trained to fight. They were tough and accustomed to the rough terrain. The Sassinids were brutal and vicious. That's why this war was a reckless war for Byzantines because their soldiers weren't trained for the kind of warfare that they faced. Their battle formations were ill-organized and prone to ambushes.

In the end, the Sassanids held Iberia and Iberia, with only one small area along the Black Sea. In the peace treaty Justinian was required to pay a massive price of 11,000 pounds. (5000 kilograms) in gold!
The Vandalic War (533-534 AD)

Justinian focused his attention towards his focus on the Central Mediterranean area. To control the region the emperor sent his army out of Constantinople under the command of his brilliant general Belisarius. The fleet then set sail Southward after conquering Methose the Greek Island. Then, from there they cruised through into the Ionian Sea, a large-mouthed channel in the Mediterranean close to Italy. Then , they headed towards Syracuse located in Sicily.

After their victory after their victory there, the Byzantine fleet headed to their next destination, the coastline of North Africa. The Vandal King, Gelimar, and his soldiers were in total shock when they Byzantines. Byzantines in the vicinity of Carthage. The Vandals as well as the Byzantines were engaged in numerous battles. The Byzantine army was highly trained, disciplined, and disciplined military force while the Vandals relied on volunteers, many of whom were untrained mercenaries. Although they were outnumbered by the Byzantine forces and lost, the Vandals were defeated likely because they were unprepared and did not have the discipline. They were also unable to keep their promises. Northern Byzantine fleet then annexed Corsica and Sardinia.

The war with the Vandals proved a remarkable win in the name of Justinian as well as the Byzantine Empire.
1. The Strategikon was a type of war manual.

The Woman who saved an Empire and took the Kingdom
Rifts at the Races

T

The date of 535 AD. Justinian had a happy marriage to intelligent and charming Theodora during the time. She was gorgeous articulate, well-spoken and persuasive, the perfect qualities to be an Empress. When Justinian was gone, Theodora ruled the Empire. She was kind to her people, and people loved her.

Justinian returned to his home after his time in the Iberian War (see above) when he realized that he needed to increase taxes He discussed it with Theodora. Being aware that citizens would be angry and discontent He and Theodora discussed the issue and decided to please the populace by organizing an event of chariot racing. The Hippodrome in Constantinople hundreds of people gathered for the event that was thrilling. The crowd was ablaze with excitement and shouted out for their teams of choice. The excitement of the crowd increased and was amplified as the chariots ran around.

Empress and Emperor watched the race from their boxes. They were cheering on the blue team. The attention of the crowd was drawn to the Emperor who was who was sitting in the corner. Being around him made them think of the new tax rates. The tensions were already at an all-time high and they began to attack the box, gnawing at it, and trying to gain entry into. A massive riot broke out in the stadium. Justinian was terrified in the presence of the thousands, and even thousands, of angry protesters. While he was a well-educated person, Justinian didn't have the courage of the warrior. The Empress Theodora However, she persuaded Justinian and his supporters in the populace to support Justinian. Theodora addressed the people and her words calmed many of them. Theodora was gorgeous and loved by the crowd. As Justinian And Theodora were kindly escorted from the stadium, they found there were thousands roaming the streets burning down buildings and demolishing anything they could. Justinian then summoned his troops and they stopped the raging. Around 3000 individuals were murdered! In the city, it was chaos.

Then, Emperor Justinian as well as Empress Theodora began the work of reconstructing

Constantinople and eventually transformed it into a beautiful city much better than prior to. Murder and Jealousy

Justinian defeated the huge islands that were off Italy However, the mainland was held by the Ostrogoths and they were ruled by the Vandals as well as the indigenous Romans. Under the dominance of Ostrogoths and Vandals there was peace until a 10-year-old boy known as Athlaric became the throne's successor. He was not old enough to be a ruler and the mother of his father, Amalasuntha was the regent.

She was beautiful friendly and kind. She also would like her son and people in the area to be educated by native Romans who were more educated as people from the Ostrogoths were in the fields of literature, sciences and the arts. However, there was a problem however. The majority of Ostrogoths were sexist towards the Romans and believed that their ancient barbarian culture could be destroyed if the Queen herself tried to woo the Romans. Therefore, they plotted and conspired against her. Therefore, she often had to take on conspirators to safeguard her son and herself from being killed. In desperate need of assistance the Queen Amalasuntha made a plea to Justinian as well as Theodora. When they first met their Queen awestruck by her beauty. Theodora was envious while she listened in silence anger to Justinian who was so kind to promise to send ambassadors.

When the emissaries set off to Italy The the Empress Theodora herself joined forces together with one, and planned against the gorgeous Queen. Theodora was terrified and anxiety about the possibility that Justinian would be divorced and marry the beautiful Amalasuntha.

The following year, the son of Amalasuntha's suffered a heart attack and later died. Since the Ostrogoths required a ruler, the Queen made her son, Theodahad, assume the throne. It was a disastrous mistake. Theodahad taken her hostage and put the woman under arrest on an island off the coast.

In the night, as Amalasuntha had been bathing, two males entered her bathroom and brutally took her life. Many believed that it was Theodahad for this savage crime, but Procopius an Medieval historian, believed the The Empress Theodora alone was the culprit in the murderous crime. Claudius, the Roman writer, Claudius could have confirmed this by writing:

"Anger arms us all.

When a powerful right hand is raging for blood, anything can be used as an axe's point.

Rage transforms anything carried into the deadly spear.

To endure for a long time, is not allowed by the laws of Fate.

The most amazing things happen at a rapid pace, and the greatest heights fall in one fell swoop.

A gorgeous woman is here.

She deserved the title of Venus as well as the utmost benefit of mortal admiration."

Today there's been no proof beyond allegations of Theodora and Theodahad. Maybe it was Both?
Conflict between Italy (535-554)

Theodahad continued to act with determination in Italy and even killed his own family members. The people who live in violence typically die through violence. The man himself was killed the next year! Following his death, a handful of unproductive kings ruled for a short time, but they were only temporary. Justinian saw an excellent opportunity to conquer Italy and so he dispatched his highly skilled general Belisarius into Belisarius to the Italian peninsula. The Ostrogoths continued to fight in a sporadic manner and on, and this war dragged on for a long time. In 554 AD, Italy was part of Justinian's huge Byzantine Empire.

Economy during the Byzantine Empire

T

He Byzantines had control over areas comprised of present-day Turkey and the Levant (countries located along the Eastern Mediterranean Sea), and the Eastern North African coast. Since they required access to Europe nations from Europe's Far East sent their caravans across the Silk Road in Mongolia and Westward. From there, the trade routes diverged SouthWest towards Nabatea (located in the present-day South Jordan) and into Constantinople. The two regions came under rule by the Byzantines. The economy was greatly boosted due to the introduction of a wide range of goods that were not available in the Mediterranean region. Silk dates, spices, dates furs, palm oil, art, silver and gold were just a few of the items that merchants offered. Constantinople was extremely prosperous because of this, and being fortunate that the city was home to an enduring government under the rule of Justinian.

The Justinian's Plague 541-542 AD

A different strain of the bacterium responsible for the Bubonic Plague that spread across The Byzantine Empire. The source is believed originate originated from imported Egyptian grain. The deadly plague killed around 25 percent of the population with a rate of approximately five thousand people every day. Even Justinian himself was affected but he survived.

The scourge impacted the entire economy during an era when Justinian was trying to pay back his debt from war, and it was massive.

Affordable Taxation

D

In order to mitigate the damage to the economy caused by this plague Justinian was able to implement a tough tax strategy to counteract the impact of the plague. He owed large amounts amount of cash to his mercenaries. He also was forced to pay for his own army. While plague-ridden corpses sat piles up in Constantinople and the towns in the areas he conquered He demanded that everyone pay their annual tax. Additionally, Justinian even required some citizens to pay the tax on their dead neighbors!

Religious Policy and Persecutions under Justinian

T

The majority of the people of the Byzantine Empire were Christian from the time of the Emperor Constantine (324-337 AD). Even though he occasionally made concessions to other religions, Justinian became more determined to ensure that all of his subjects follow Christianity. The exile of pagan educators was even a factor from Athens. Also in Asia Minor, he dispatched Christian teachers to actively try to convert population in the region. Rights of Jewish population were restricted and Justinian also attempted to interfere with the synagogues of their people. Justinian also resented those who opposed conversion, as did that of Samarians from the Levant.

Legacy

B

At when Justinian died at the time of his death, at the time of his death, Byzantine Empire consisted of:

* Anatolia (current-day Turkey)
* Greece and the countries immediately North of there
* Coastal regions that run along the Adriatic Sea
* Italy
* Corsica and Sardinia
* Carthage
* Today's Tunisia
* Coastal countries of North Africa
* Northern Egypt
* The Levant
* Syria

From the East and into the West

C

civilizations between the 7th and the 8th century were centered around religions and beliefs. In the Arabian Peninsula, trade routes propagated the message about new faiths. The new religions spread via trade routes, and eventually to the Christian World of the Byzantine Empire. The 6th century was the time when the first era of the religion and in the ancient Mecca, the city Mecca, paganism flourished. The main belief was known as animism. The belief of animism is that existence was under the control of the natural forces of goodwill and demon spirits. But another religion was born within the Mid East- that of Islam.

Islam

M
uhammad Uhammad Mecca in modern-day Saudi Arabia, is the first founder of Islam. The central message he preached was simple and substituted the animistic belief of various gods. Islam is a religion that believes in one god known as Allah. Furthermore, he declared that all people are equal before the God of Allah. When Muhammad propagated the different religion, he as well as his followers were initially persecuted. According to the biographer of Muhammad, Ibn Ishaq:

"They got angry against Muhammad the Prophet Muhammad - foolish men who called him a fool and insulted him. They also were able to accuse him...However The Messenger (Muhammad) was able to announce the words that Allah directed him to announce."

Muhammad was exiled and was eventually settled in Medina, South of Mecca. He gained more followersand then returned to Mecca, his hometown, Mecca. Then , he and his men defeated Mecca under the banner of Islam. Muslim territories expanded until they took control of the whole Arabian Peninsula.

The Caliphate of Rashidun (632-661)

A
fter Muhammad died, Islam did not die with him. It expanded Northward and also along to the Northern shores from Africa during the time of successors to Muhammad. The succession of Muhammad was not without controversy the followers of his were divided in two distinct groups. the Sunni's and Shi'ites. Most Muslims who were Sunni under the guidance by Abu Bakr, the first Caliph.

Muslims were growing in number and pushed for expansion in the era of the Rashiduns. They shifted Northward and fought over Byzantine territories that lie along the Eastern Mediterranean. The Byzantine Empire was able to lose a large portion of its territory however, the Empire managed to keep most of Anatolia (Turkey).

The Muslims were able to settle in their homelands of Levant, Syria and Eastward towards Persia (current-day Iran). They then annexed two nations that are now called Afghanistan as well as Turkmenistan. The capital city of the Rashidun Caliphate was later relocated to Mecca in Damascus, Syria.

Islam spread to other parts of the world and spread Southward into the ex- Byzantine areas of the present-day Egypt as well as a small portion from Ethiopia as well as Libya. Then, in North Africa, they nearly destroyed all Berber nomads.

The Umayyad Caliphate (661-750)

T

the Umayyads came to the rescue by the Rashiduns. Afterward, an internal war began between the Sunnis in the era of ibn Yazid and the Shi'ites under al-Husayn Ali. The issue was once again the right to succession.
The Battle of Karbala 680 AD

The battle of the century was marked by the betrayal. Al-Husayn Ali, Muhammad's grandson was fighting Yazid. Al-Husayn was assured of his supporters by a large number of followers before they were to meet him at Karbala. As he reached Karbala the city, there were only one or two followers who stood with him.

Yazid as the Umayyad Caliph had an army of 5,000. They took on Husayn Ali's small group of around 100 soldiers. Al-Husayn's entire family joined to fight for his cause. Al-Husayn Ali was executed together with his son al-Abbas ibn Ali and his newborn son.

Every year, Shia Muslims commemorate this tragedy in Karbala at this Day of Ashura, the date is set by the ancient Muslim calendar. The site also houses a well-known site of worship and the Shia are known to make pilgrimages to the holy place. Shi'ites around the world pray and write poems on this historic event that altered the direction in Islamic history:

"The battle between swords and the tussle of souls

The song was played by dawn, following the darkness of night.

Many thousands of people struggle for the dark to prevail

A little less than one hundred warriors from the light.

The tenth day of Muharram on the sands of Karbala

This morning, a battle bloody battles continued to rage

In a few hours, the length of centuries is apparent.

A sorrow that occurs when young children have reached the age of."

In the reign of Caliph Yazid as well as his successors more part of the Mediterranean world was conquered, thereby expanding to include the Muslim territories to encompass the present-day countries that are Algeria, Morocco, and across the Straits of Gibraltar into Portugal and Spain. The Caliphate included greater than 5 million square miles (13 million square kilometers).

In the meantime, Europe

W
The Caliphates were expanding their territory in their territory to Mid East, across North Africa and eventually into Hispania (Spain) and into Spain, the Europeans were in control of Francia (France), Germania and the Greek peninsula and the Slavic territories, and from the Eastern European kingdoms.

The "Do-Nothing" Kings of Francia

I
In the 6th century, Francia had been part of the Western Holy Roman Empire. Francia was first colonized by the Germanic tribe known as the Franks. The revered Christian leader, Clovis, ruled the region. Prior to the 511 death of his father, Clovis divided the country into 4 parts each one of which was managed by the sons of his heir. The sons, however, were

sluggish and self-indulgent enjoying the wealth that were reaped by Clovis when he established this well-organized and prosperous nation. They were not interested in an effective system of government. Due to the utter negligence in the "Do-Nothing" Kings, other members of their court were required to manage the country. In relation to these weak rulers the ancient historian Einhardt stated:

"Nothing is left for the King. He had to live with his title of king with his flowing locks and a long beard."

"The Hammer Strikes!

When Francia was in a state of discontent amid the "Do-Nothing" Kings while The "Moors," (Spanish Muslims) represented the Umayyad caliphate in Iberia. The Moors were then pushed to the East and threatened the border of Francia. A brave court official known as"the mayor" Palace Charles Martel Charles Martel - rose up and declared his intention to stop the march from the Moors Eastward towards Christian Europe. His name "Martel" is a reference to "hammer," and that became his nickname. Martel was handed on through his family.

The "Hammer" built a powerful army, which was organized in the structure of feudalism. His knights were mounted who were heavily armored and they took an oath of loyalty to their commander. Being aware of the fact that Moors were in the process of mobilizing along his Western frontier of Francia, Martel created an alliance of forces from Europe.
Battle of Tours 732 AD Battle of Tours 732 AD

Martel's powerful army fought off the Moorish cavalry in The city of Tours in Francia. Despite the fact that the Franks were only feet soldiers, they shrewdly stood their ground. With a clever plan, Martel split off a small force that racked up at the Umayyad base camp in the hinterlands of the city. When the Moors were aware of this, many of them left the battlefield to guard the treasure they kept inside their camps. Only half of Moorish cavalry remained on the battlefield.

This trick was successful. In the wake of the massive number of Franks that were now threatening them and the rest of the Moors were also able to leave the field and seemed to be heading back to their camps to rest for the night. Thus, Martel and his men remained for the night, hoping they would fight next day.

The Medieval Muslim Chronicle, The Mozarabid Chronicle says:

"...the Europeans were able to see the canopies and tents of the Arabs set up like they had been the previous day. Unaware that they were empty, and believing that in them are Saracen (Moorish) forces preparing to battle They sent officers, and were surprised to find that all the Ishmaelite (Moorish) soldiers had gone. They did indeed flee in silence at night in a tight groupings, and returned home to their country."

This is why the Muslims had fled in peace to sleep. It was a victory that Christian Europe was possibly one of the greatest. But it was also the case that the Southern region in Francia remains under Umayyad control. This region must be dealt with in the future.

The Carolingian Empire

F

The kingdom of Rancia was decentralized that was divided into a number of smaller, independent Germanic tribal regions. Pepin Short Short had the greatest power as the Mayor in Francia. Palace in Francia in the early 8th century. It was Pope Stephen II knew of Pepin's ability to fight and urged him to expel Lombards as they were intruding onto the Papal estate in Italy. Pepin stated that he would be a good response should the Pope was to appoint Pepin as King of the Franks.

Pepin succeeded and Pepin was successful and the Pope declared Pepin as King of the Franks in 751 AD. In exchange for the pope's favour, Pepin later set aside the territory of Rome to the Pope to be crowned in 754 AD and gave the pope authority to govern the territory. This area is now called"the "Papal State."

Charlemagne (768-814 AD)

C

harlemagne was believed to have stood over six feet tall, an impressive muscular figure that attracted admiration and attention. Charlemagne imagined an ideal Frankish Kingdom where it would be able to create a sophisticated culture of education, Christianity and beauty. Charlemagne was a master orator. He was charming and charismatic and his people loved him. Charlemagne was a ruler with the brother of his, Carloman.

The Meddling Pope

P

epin passed away before he was able to completely take control of the area close to Rome from the king Desiderius as well as his Lombards. When a new Pope came into his post in the year 2000, the Lombards took on the new Pope. Similar to his predecessor Stephen II, Pope Stephen II appealed to Charlemagne along with Carloman to solve the issue. They responded , but the mother of their sons, Bertrada, suggested a more radical approach that Pepin used. If her sons were to marry to Desiderius the clan, that would create an alliance. They were in agreement, and so was Desiderius. Carloman was able to decide to get married Gerberga and Desiderata would be married to Charlemagne. The wedding took place in the year 770 AD as well as the Lombard dispute was resolved.

But the Pope was shocked! He thought that Medieval Kings were to marry beautiful women from the same race as they and ethnicity. In the end, King was allowed to have concubines but weren't elevated to rank of royalty. In a loud voice, he informed the Frankish King know what he thought:

"I am awash with grief when I learned that Desiderius ruler of the Lombards is seeking to wed his child to one of your relatives, which is clearly a sinister suggestion...this Lombard race, perfidious and unclean...What absurdity to think that kings with such a prestigious reputation can be relegated to this horrible degrading!"

The popes were powerful agents during the Medieval World, so it was not wise to not follow by their decisions. To please to the Pope, Charlemagne divorced poor Desiderata and went back to Lombardy. Carloman his brother was murdered or killed within a short time, and Gerberga went back to Lombardy also.

2 There was a rumor the possibility that Charlemagne killed Carloman but this has never been proved.

Wars and Lombardy 773 AD

A
It is possible to predict that the king Desiderius was furious over the insulting act which led to his declaration of war. Charlemagne then gathered his troops and made his way over the icy peaks in the Alps to take on Lombardy. He lost thousands of troops horses, equipment and even horses but he was able to defeat the king Desiderius. When Charlemagne returned to his home and was greeted by the Lombards regularly threw a fit at the Popes as well as the indigenous people in the Italian peninsula. In many cases, Charlemagne had to return. It took close to 20 years before the Lombards had to leave and relocate to Northern Italy.

Wars within the East

C

Harlemagne was adamant about the Germanic territories in Saxony that were situated within the Eastern boundaries to his kingdom. They were pagans who were dedicated to their gods of nature who they built bizarre stone pillars with foreign text. With aplomb, Charlemagne attacked them with his armored army that flung their swords and brutally pounded the slain soldiers in bloody combats.

Reconquistration of Saxony 773-804
The "Wolf"
W

idukind led the Saxons. In his Saxon language, "Widukind" means wolf. The tribe of his barbarians originated in the Anglo-Saxon areas that are located in Scandinavia and he sought out the lush, fertile land that lie in Germania and Francia which is why the tribe and its members moved into the lands. Charlemagne was also interested in that region which is why both he and Widukind were involved in many battles over the territory. Although it took close to 30 years,

Charlemagne had a superior combat force and won. Widukind began to dislike the Franks particularly when Widukind noticed their uniforms and observed their nobles in dresses and ruffles.

The Anglo-Saxon Chronicles written during the Middle Ages, he was mentioned as having stated "Where is a big Hell large enough to accommodate Franks? Franks?"

Saxonia was the name given to what is now Eastern France and most of Germany. The region was split into 4 parts:

* Austrasia
* Eastphalia
* Westphalia
* Engria

Charlemagne took over the whole region and abandoned fortresses to protect his authority. Every time he went out to fight in other campaigns however, certain Saxon states revolted. He had to be constantly returning. The goal of Charlemagne was to integrate all of the area into Francia. However, these

Saxons were tough warriors who would like to return the territory to its roots.

At the conclusion of the Saxon campaigns, Charlemagne came to appreciate the intelligence and culture of the people. He enacted a code of law known as the "Lex Saxonum" which gave civil rights to the people as well as allowing the Saxons to govern their own sub-kingdoms. Charlemagne is also known as a committed Christian and in the manner that was typical of his time - demanded that the Saxons change their religion. In actual fact, their famous chief, Widukind, was one of the first to convert.

As time passed, Saxons and Franks came together to form alliances. At times, however, a few provinces tried to take back control of small regions in order to create "mini-kingdoms."

Reconquista of the Avars 788-803 AD
Campaign to stop the Pannonian Avars

T
The Avars are nomadic tribal groups who are believed to have come out of their homeland

in the Mongolian region. Early historians referred to them as the Huns but they are believed to be a distinct tribe than the one of Attila. Charlemagne and his skilled warriors took on their land, that was situated in a few of the regions that comprise today's Hungary, Austria, Slovakia and Serbia. It was situated just to the east from what was then the Frankish Kingdom.

To conquer the region, Charlemagne had recruited help from the strong Saxon kingdoms. It was the year 788 AD. Due to the Saxon rebellion and an Lombard rebellion and a Lombard rebellion, it took Charlemagne several years to defeat his opponents in the Avar Confederation. In the year 803, he was successful.

The war in the West

S
the pain, also known as "Hispania" at the time and is and was under Muslim control. The group, which was comprised from the Moors as well as the Muladi tribes, originated origins from North Africa and had occupied parts of

Hispania. The legend of the great Charlemagne was spread to the Muslims in Hispania as well as the ruler of Hispania, Abd ar-Rahman I of the Umayyad Dynasty was in search of his help to resolve the constant conflicts in the area. In the return, Abd ar-Rahman offered homage and offered to be a vassal of Francia. This offered a chance for Charlemagne to increase the size of the boundaries of his Carolingian Empire, and Charlemagne accepted. In response to a requests by Abd ar-Rahman, Charlemagne dispatched two troops to traverse the Pyrenees and conquer the area.

The Basques at Roncesvalles Pass

One of his contingents and the other was commanded by Roland the nephew of Charlemagne who was a great leader and legendary commander. They first had to traverse the high mountain peaks of the Pyrenees to get into Hispania as a whole.

In 778, during the 778 year at Roncesvalles Pass, Roland encountered an armed force of fierce fighting which occupied the frontier that separated Hispania as well as Francia. In terms of the norms of war, it was not an incredibly brutal battle, but Basques were bloodthirsty and brutal warriors. In the fight, Roland died. In the Medieval poem, called the Song of Roland, it states that one of the enemies soldiers saw the insignia of the Franks on his chest...

"he hit him with a full force smashing bone, steel and skull. In the back of his head, his eyes, he beat and then he dragged him to his feet."
The war against the Moors 779-713 AD

In Hispania the war dragged on. In 797 797, the Franks were able to take control of Barcelona. Charlemagne was able to have his son Louis of Aquitaine, to besiege the Southern part of Hispania to protect the Franks. They fought bravely with the small emir al-Hakam. In the later years of Charlemagne's rule, in 813 AD the king capitulated.

Coronation of Charlemagne

A

It was a shock when It was a shock when Pope Leo III named Charlemagne Emperor of Rome. In this way, Charlemagne was believed to be the legitimate successor to Constantine. Charlemagne was not comfortable with this title as it could be interpreted as a way to end any rule of Irene Irene, the Empress from Constantinople. The Empress was also the ruler of what was left in the Byzantine Empire. But, Charlemagne accepted the role. But for the rest of his existence, Charlemagne attempted to stay clear of the Pope. It was 799 AD.

Death

I

In in the year 814 AD, Charlemagne died of the disease of pleurisy. The people loved him because he restored peace in their land. In the wake of his demise one monk remarked:

"From the regions that the sun rises to the western shores of the ocean the people are weeping as well as wailing...O Christ, you who control the heavenly hosts provide a serene home for Charles within your kingdom."

III

Feudalism: Europeans Segmented

The 10th century was when Kingdoms were established in Europe in Europe and Great Britain. Feudalism was the way in through which kingdoms could be governed. A kingdom was comprised of:

The King is the ruler of the kingdom

The Barons were the ones who leased their land to the King. Their estates were referred to as "manors," and they were the executors of their estate.

The Knights were professional soldiers who guarded and defended the manor, Baron, and the family of his. They were paid well and were given land to cultivate farms as a reward in exchange for their work.

The Serfs The serfs often referred to "villeins," were granted an area on the manor and they used it for food as well as other services for knights in addition to for their own and other members of the manor as needed. The serfs were extremely poor.

Knights, and The Code of Chivalry

T
The ideals of honor, dedication and unending courage were taught to the boys of the ages who enrolled in the training program in order to be knights.

The Book of Chivalry by Geoffroi de Charny is a good example:

"Those who are determined to attain great value and who, because of their burning desire to succeed and achieve that honor...do not think about the pain they endure and turn it into a great pleasure. It is indeed good to be able to carry out impressive acts because those who achieve high levels of achievement are not able to get exhausted or bored with it. Consequently, the higher they go more, the less they believe they've accomplished; this is due to the joy that they experience in trying to attain higher levels. It is also a great feeling to be doing these acts, because the more one accomplishes it, the less one can be self-confident, and it is always apparent that there's plenty to accomplish."

Knights carried chain mail as well as thick armors, and helmets as well as carried weapons and shields. One of the weapons they decided to carry included a lance broadsword, battle axe and daggers. Their armor shielded against the sharp thrusts of the weapons of their adversaries, however they were so heavy the knights needed to be carried on their horses! A lot of horses were also equipped with armor.

Tournaments

J

Outer-staging tournaments were played on the grounds of the castle at the manor. They were a method that the knights worked on hone their skills and entertained their fellow knights during peacetime. The celebrations were awe-inspiring. Lady and Lord were often present and, obviously large crowds of fans who chanted. In many ways, it was an event of sport however, it was more violent.

Knighthood's contribution to the Middle Ages

T
The introduction of knights operating in accordance with the ethical code of conduct improved the character of the war. In some ways, this was beneficial as it helped to reduce the brutality of conflict that was sadistically violent. Knighthood also brought more planning and organization into fights. In another way it was a way to transform conflicts into noble pursuits through the kingdoms could believe that they have redressed an actual or imagined wrong. Of course it was just determined to conquer, regardless of the legal right to conquer. The majority of wars in the Middle Ages were to satisfy the need to be a dominant force. Other wars were fought to defend motives, that is, to safeguard the integrity of a region.

The Castle

C
astles became sophisticated in the 10th century. At first, they were wooden fortresses set on hillsides, with moats and walls. Moats smelled unpleasant because they were

littered with organic waste such as human waste!

In the past castles were built from carefully cut stone. Within the walls was a large courtyard with stores, jails, and storage areas for food, water and weapons. There were also cabins for servants. Barracks were also available for the residents in the manor. They were used to protect during a lengthy siege. The center of the complex castle was an important structure known as the keep. The Lord and Lady of the manor resided there, along with members of the knights' families. The castle's top walls were large and guarded by knights. A drawbridge was elevated and lower to allow or block access.

The Grounds

T

The area around the castle was home to the serfs, as well as areas allocated for hunter's preserves and grazing areas for sheep and cattle farms, and forests which were cut for wood when needed. The house for the serfs was quite simple with a single or two-story without windows. There was a fireplace at the heart of the hut , as well as there was a gap in the roof, which allowed the smoke out. The floor was constructed from dirt. Furniture and bedding were primitive.

The serfs were equipped with tools for working the landscape. In the early days they used a simple tool. The plow was developed together with collars for horses and Oxen. In the 11th century, agriculture was upgraded with the utilization of natural fertilizers, windmills and water to provide irrigation for the crops and grinding stones and grains. This is how the gristmill became a reality.

The Minstrels

T

Minstrels sung the most popular ballads of the time. The songs told stories about the real and fantastical incidents. A majority of the people were unable to read, and it was a method of ensuring that the actions of the knights and kings were circulated throughout the kingdom. The minstrels frequently exaggerated the details to make King's appearance appear as superheroes. The ballads might be offensive or utterly inaccurate. The minstrel would use whatever could entertain or convey the strongest emotion, whether it was joy or sorrow.

Sung to honor the lady who was the victim of a lover's death:
Bonnie Barbara Allen

"...And slowly gradually raise her up,

and slowly and slowly, slowly, he left him

and sighing she decided she couldn't stay.

The death of life had taken him away.

She'd only travelled more than two miles,

As she listened to the death knell sounding,

And every squeak dead-bell made,

It was crying"Woe for Barbara Allen!

Oh, mother, Make my bed!

O, thin and soft!

My love has died today for me,

I will be his last victim the next day."

Education

I
In Europe in the past, feudalism was the foundational element of society during the 9th and 15th century. Knights and the fighting force were functionally unliterate, as were the majority of the population. In the time that Charlemagne was in power

in the 9th Century many of the priests in the parish couldn't write or read. Because of the influence of more academic cultures, such as those in Greece and Rome, there was a desire for education. Charlemagne established educational centers in monasteries to allow clergymen to be educated and be able teach others using the Bible. The trend continued through into the Middle Ages.
Writing

Writing was certainly there however it was mostly crude text written onto oil skins of monks. Monks meticulously copied the Scriptures employing their Old Roman style of writing. However, the words and sentences were all spelled out and there weren't any capitals. The writing was virtually unreadable. Foreign affairs and trade needed an element of effective communication, and this type of writing was almost unusable. In the 10th century, it was upgraded. Pictures and capital letters depicting the themes of the documents were meticulously painted.

Parchment was later substituted for oil skin. To honor the nobles, gold-plated Bible covers that depicted the words, images and symbols were made.

Additionally, there was a dire need for a program of study so that European people could acquire the abilities needed to create an enlightened civilization. Studying in the disciplines of medicine, sciences, math and religion could help to raise to the Mediterranean world.
Medicine

Avicenna was Avicenna was a Persian medical doctor, philosopher, and Astronomer. He lived between 980 and 1037 AD. Concerning medicine, he stated: "In medicine we ought to understand the reasons for sickness and health. Within the Canon of Medicine, he gave useful medical advice to the general population. For instance, he provided tips on the purification of drinking water.

"Snow water and the water that comes that is melted ice are rough in texture. When they are pure and free of the admixture of harmful substances, the water is healthy and safe. Water from snowwater or melted ice is dangerous for people suffering with neuritis. Boiling makes the water healthy."
Science

In the year 1100 the first mariner's compass was invented in China. In 1187, it was revived in Europe in 1187, and later in Scandinavia in the year 1300. The people had realized that the mineral lodestone is aligned in an orientation of North-South. Then, they carefully plotted the four directions using a dial and then added precise measurements of the angles between. This was a valuable instrument for navigation on the sea , and even on land. The plots of land within the manor estates could be better measured, which proved useful in determining the dimensions of the land parcels that were assigned to each serf and knight.

Architecture

M

athematics is the basis architects utilized
to plan out secular and church buildings. In
the 2nd century, they incorporated a style
typical from that of the Later Roman
Empire. This is why it's called
"Romanesque." Its buildings featured
arched arches that were rounded and with
shorter steep roofs. The walls were huge
and heavy. There were very few windows,
with one window that was that were used
to permit an gun barrel to protrude. The
walls required support, and half-circle
structures were built in the vicinity of
three or four walls. Arches with pointed
ends weren't added until later.

Columns were basic, but there were times
when they had intricate carvings on the
top of the column. The stylized foliage and
simple geometric designs were employed
to decorate the interior and exterior
columns. A "barrel vault" was common to

the period. It was an extruding semi-circular or circular stone structure. In the middle was a very attractive stained glass windows.

Art

S

Tone reliefs were created over the portals. Since Europe was Christian the artwork featured religious themes , like the depictions of Christ as well as saints and apostles. Animals were also included in combination with Biblical stories such as Noah's Ark. Sometimes there were political figures incorporated such as the King and Queen. Each figure featured intricate stylistic patterns, and sometimes even script.

The paintings and frescoes that were on walls were not uncommon, but they were often destroyed by dampness.

In addition to the earlier illuminated manuscripts, public and church structures featured tapestries. The church vestments and clothes were embellished in intricately designed patterns. The tapestries could depict a historical event, such as a major battle. The threads of silver and gold were commonly used, and the tapestries were costly. Nowadays, these products are irreplaceable.

Chapter 14: William The Conqueror 1028-1087 Ad

William was also referred to as "William the Bastard" due to his status as the unlegitimate son of Robert I. and Herleva. Robert was Duke of Normandy. Normandy was founded by the "Norsemen (also known as "Normans" who came from Norway. Normandy became an English vassal state within France in the year 1028.

England in the period of its time was occupied by Celts, Normans, Danes and Anglo-Saxons. It was administered by Edward "the Confessor" who was an Anglo-Saxon. William was the cousin of King Edward. Dukes from Normandy were part of royal family of England and were mostly Anglo-Saxons.

After the demise of his father, in the year 1035 AD, William became Duke of Normandy. But he was just seven years old at the time and was under the supervision and security of his family until he reached old enough to be. In the whole Middle Ages, internecine warfare was widespread. Family members and friends of members of the extended royal families often killed one another or their supporters in an effort to take over the Duchy of Normandy or the throne of the monarch of England. Five people who were guarding William from being killed were believed to have been murdered. One of them even killed in front of William's bedchamber!

When William reached the age of majority to take over his father's Duchy of Normandy and the chaos began to erupt. Many of his relatives protested against William's taking on the title of Duke suggesting that William's ineligibility was enough reason to remove his title.

One was the Countess of Brionne, Guy. Guy of Brionne formed an army of over 25,000 soldiers and was able to take on William and his tiny military group.

The Battle of Val-es-Dunes 1047

A

In the valley of es-Dunes In the valley of es-Dunes Guy in the valley of es-Dunes, Count Guy Brionne and William were at war. It was a bloody fight but William suffered defeat because he was overwhelmed and was almost attacked by Guy's troops. William himself changed his horse and rode off to seek assistance by the French King Henry I. Henry himself was among William's defenders, and he swiftly put together a force of 10,000 soldiers before racing back to William. During the this battle the King Henry was not seated on his horse, but was protected from one of his troops. Henry was barely saved from the death. Guy's men shook in fear when the tide changed and they fled toward the river. William, Henry and their men resisted the attack. After the day, a mass of bodies floated down the river, obstructing the flow and terrorizing inhabitants of the countryside.

Battle of Mortemer 1054: The Battle of Mortemer 1054

W

William gained many admirers throughout Normandy with the nobles. But, as William increased his strength his strength increased, he faced enemies. Many of these enemies included his own nobles and with whom William was forced to engage in several battles. The most significant shake-up in Northern France was caused by the deceit by the king Henry I. Henry was very frightened as William became more powerful. The King later allied himself with William's enemies.

William was still able to count on the support of influential Norman nobles such as Robert the The Count of Eu, Roger of Mortemer, William de Warenne and Hugh of Gournay to help him to hold back the King and his troops. William and his men were victorious in the initial battles.

King Henry led the last group located on his Eastern side of the river.When he learned that the French troops had suffered significant losses, he decided to withdraw. Duke William had won a clear victory, and a large number of the nobles of the enemy changed their allegiances to him and joined his.

Battle of Varaville 1057

I

In an effort to lessen the power of William in order to limit the power of William, in an attempt to limit the power of William, King Henry was able to join forces to the powerful Countess of the Duchy of Anjou, Geoffrey Martel and other nobles. The King normally was in opposition to Martel however - in the interest of enhancing his power over Normandy the King allied himself together with Geoffrey Martel. Then Geoffrey and King were able to invade Eastern Normandy. It was noted that the Dives River at Varaville was highly prone to the tides. When King Henry and

Martel's troops were traversing this river, the water abruptly flooded in and the first part of the invading army was swept away by the river. William immediately took advantage of this to defeat Henry's other troops by defeating them. In the end, William won another victory.

Crises in England

D

during the reign of King Edward, the Earls who governed the different territories of England increased their power substantially. Since they were wealthy and had vast tracts of land, which included numerous manors and estates, the influence they had over the King was significantly increased. In 1053 AD the Lord Harold Godwinson and his brothers practically ruled the majority of the Earldoms in England.

King Edward was a long-running battle to keep control of the greedy and headstrong nobles. He also tried to manage Scotland

and Wales that were invading into the English counties.

Edward was fed up with the battles for power. He was in alliance with Harold Godwinson, an alliance which could give him a tenuous grip on the English throne. In the year 1065 Edward would spend most of the time hunting, and let the Earls rule the kingdom.

The Succession Conflict

T

The the Kings of England traditionally choose who will succeed them as the heirs of the English throne. The heirs are usually selected from their direct descendants. Edward was a single parent, so he was able to choose from his family members. Edward however, chose two heirs at various times throughout his life! It is possible that he was unaware of the first one, as there were other matters. A historical document from in the Middle Ages indicates that Edward picked his Earl

Harold Godwinson. There was no formal proof of the promise, but Harold announced that he would become his successor as the monarch. Harold was the son of Edward's wife but was not a royal blood carrier. The descendant from the Viking King of 1016, Harald Hardrada, claimed that his name should be given the throne. However, he was not the Edward's descendant. Edward had one close relative that was qualified as Edgar who was known as the "Atheling." It was believed that Edgar was the"heir apparent," and that's why the word "Atheling" signifies. The problem with this assumption was that Edgar was young and sick. William the Conqueror was, however the cousin of Edward and claimed the right to the throne claiming it was because Edward was a promise to him for the throne in 1051. There was no evidence in writing of this.

The Agreement between Harold and William Agreement with William

As per William Poitier's medieval historical document, William rescued Harold Godwinson from prison following an accident on a ship in 1064. In return, William asked Harold to give up all rights related to the throne. Harold was willing to do so. In reference to this incident, William said:

"Through the use of his (Harold's) hand, the man became my vassal, and then with his own hand , he made me his unconditional pledge regarding the Kingdom of England."
This was recorded through the Bayeux Tapestry that was embroidered following the Battle of Hastings.

In 1066, when the King Edward passed away in the year 1066 The King's Council, called a "Witan," decided to make the Earl Harold the king, mainly due to the fact that the Earl was extremely powerful. Harold did not make any reference to the agreement he had made with William and was later crowned the King Harold II.

The Battle of Stamford Bridge -September 1066AD

H
Arald Hardrada opposed the Witan's choice, and he declared war against the King Harold Godwinson. The two armies of the King fought each other in one-on-one battle on the Stamford bridge that crossed the Denwent River. The troops under Hardrada were in a defensive position by making an "shield wall" against the English forces that roared through the bridge. The term "shield wall" is a type of military formation that sees mounted soldiers are grouped with shields next to one another, creating an "wall" made of shields. Godwinson's men, who were determined, fought the Hardrada for several hours, but they were unable to breach. In the end, Godwinson's men fought King Harold and his troops massacred the bulk of Harrada's army. Harald himself perished in the fight.

Not so Long is the King's reign Battle of Hastings: Battle of Hastings -October 1066 AD

K

in Harold and his men forced survivors of Harold forced the survivors of Battle of Stamford to join together with his own soldiers. The large army had to move South away from Stamford Bridge in order to fight William who had seized the island in the harbor of Pevensey in the English Channel. To stop the progress of William, Harold conducted a forced march of 27 miles per hour. In the varied terrain of Hastings both forces were able to meet. Harold ordered his troops to form a tight line over a hill with the shield wall. The flanks of his men were guarded on the other side by trees and the front was surrounded by marshes. This was the ideal spot to secure.

William was able to divide his troops into 3 divisions. The first was the archers, but his supply of arrows was exhausted before the time. Then he sent an additional group of spearmen. They had no luck to break through the Harold's wall. Then William made his Normans make a fake retreat. William was known for being a clever commander who would often surprise his adversaries with unexpected actions and so the fake retreat was an effective strategy.

Convinced that victory was close imminent, Harold's men rushed into the front. In a shocking twist, William was unseated from his horse. Rumors circulated among Normans that he was killed. William was healthy and alive. To keep the Normans in retreat, William boldly stood upon the ground and waved his helmet up in the air. After they were able to see William his helmet, the Normans changed their course and fought back against Harold's army with ferocious force.

The battle raged on all day. When sunset was settling in an bright orange skies

Harold got stuck with an arrow which caused a puncture in his eye, and then pierced the brain. In the Bayeux Tapestry showed that occurrence.

In battle, William then took the standard of Harold and presented his standard to the Pope to show of his victory in battle . He also sought the Pope's blessing. At the time the king required an ecclesiastical endorsement.

King Edgar Atheling Perhaps?

T
The Witan was clear against William's accession to the throne and so they elected the sickly teenage boy Edgar as the heir for the position of king. But, Edgar hadn't yet had his accession confirmed by the Pope as had William yet. It could have helped his case to receive the blessing by his Archbishop Canterbury who is the prelate in charge in England however, the Archbishop had a favorable opinion of Edgar instead. The Pope had not yet

replied. To increase his chances of claiming the throne William began his march towards London. In the process the king took on the English army near Southwark and then landed just outside London. When he learned that William was actually right in front of London's capital, Archbishop retracted his support for Edgar and backed William instead. The Archbishop then informed to the Pope that he was supporting William.

Coronation of William I, King William I

P

Ope Alexander II later granted his assent. William was named William I on the 25th of December 1066. The royal family of today begins their genealogies back to William the Conqueror.

Foreign Kings as well as English Earls Revolt

A

Following the time that William was crowned as King, it seemed obvious that he wouldn't let the Earls to enjoy the power they enjoyed under the previous regimes that included Edward the Confessor as well as Harold Godwinson. These Earls were ruling England. They were all corrupt and had passed directives that favor prelates as well as other wealthy families that bribed them. King William was aware that this could destroy a nation.

As the Earls did, Scotland and Denmark also wanted control. Both were looking to have William to be removed as a means of allowing them to strike Britain. Scotland was a rugged country that was not as affluent for agriculture while its ports were not navigable. The rich fields and ports with warm water Britain are a particular advantage in boosting trade. Denmark is a tiny country was home to a rapidly growing population and desired to grow.

One of the most significant of the wars William had to resolve in relation to his control over the Earls as well as the defense from Scotland and England included:

* Malcom III of Scotland 1067
* Earl Waltheof 1069
* King Sweyn of Denmark 1069
* Earl Ralph of Norfolk 1075
* Earl Roger of Hereford 1075
* King Cnut of Denmark
* Earl Morcar 1087

All of the adversaries seemed to be aware of William's superior military capabilities. The enemies of William were defeated and were forced to bow to William the King. William.

The "Doomesday" Book!

W

William ruled with his iron his. He had heard from the immense wealth of the Earls and was aware that they were also taking the power of serfs and knights who worked in their vast manors. Many of the wealthy owned huge properties in Normandy and the surrounding counties.

William was also burdened by post-war debt, and did not want to send the country's Treasury into bankruptcy. The previous King of England were inept when it came to valuing the land, and didn't have any sort of real-time census. The king must also be aware of who they were and what property that the landowners of the kingdom were able to acquire. They were the ones responsible for paying taxes.

King William later called an advisory council, and had them create Doomesday Book. Doomesday Book. The name was often called "Doomesday," because of its nature. It was a popular book. Doomesday Book wasn't popular, obviously, but it did help to keep the English Treasury in good state.

1 A weir is a tiny dam-like structure that is built in waterways to catch fish.

Data recorded

E
The size of the shire was about 120 acres. These plots of land were part of the manor that was governed by barons or Earls. In the Domesday Book meticulously included the items and equipment within the shires. This included, for instance the number of plows as well as horses, water and windmills, as well as fishing weirs1. It also included the land held by bishops or abbots, priors and the King only (e.g. Hunting preserves).

The Domesday Book also had several chapters that recorded the amount of arable land land that was not inhabited forests, rivers ports and other similar. The towns were classified differently. Dues were imposed for specific crafts and trades, as were shops, therefore the records were kept for these as well.

Rebellious Robert!

R

obert Obert Robert Curthose was King William's firstborn son. He was argumentative, obstinate and had passive aggressive tendencies. He would often incite his brothers Richard and younger William to violently retaliate. When the King intervened Robert often blamed his brothers for starting the fighting. Robert's brothers were extremely displeased with him and often came up with naughty ways to avenge themselves. The boys would throw objects at Robert and he would do the same. In one instance that was mentioned by historians of the medieval period that Robert's brothers threw the contents of a chamber over his head! The King was aware of Robert as well as his other sons well, and so Robert's brothers weren't punished. Robert was furious at his father. At one point, Robert plotted with some of his naive friends to take over Rouen's Cathedral at Rouen! After spotting this sinister plot the King William was ordered to arrest Robert. Robert was also very dismayed that his family's conflict was now known to the world.

In the hopes that Robert was able to mature after being given a significant obligation, his father granted him the control of his County of Maine in 1063. Maine is located situated in Northern France, was a vassal-ruled state, governed by English. Robert was an unprofessional administrator and was unable to control the state in 1069. The French then exiled Robert as well as the Norman officials. Then , they put an French baron over Maine. Robert did not want to accept responsibility as he blamed his dad! He was very young.

Robert Curthose continued to cause chaos and conflicts everywhere the he went. King William felt compelled to leave estate in his will however, he only left his Duchy of Normandy to him. King William was then able to announce that his heir to throne of England was a the young William.

Robert Goes Crusading 1096

D

In the period when Robert Curthose was Duke of Normandy in the years when Robert Curthose was Duke of Normandy, a pastor named Peter the Hermit walked during the time of Robert Curthose's Dukeship through the French countryside, calling on able-bodied men to liberate the holy Land from Palestine of the Muslims. Peter's call was further emphasized with the help of Alexius I, the Byzantine Emperor, who wrote a letter for pope Urban II, begging assistance from the destruction caused by the Seljuk Turks, the Muslim tribes that controlled both Turkey as well as Turkey's Holy Land. Seljuk Turks Seljuk Turks constantly harassed and targeted the Christian pilgrims who came to Jerusalem as well as the holy places. Robert, the adventurous Robert was the first to respond to the request.

As you can imagine, he didn't do very well during his journey into Palestine, the Holy Land for the First Crusade. He had squandered his money in the process and was suffering from indigence before he arrived in Palestine. Then , he loaned his Duchy of Normandy in Normandy to the brother of his William.

Conclusion

We hope that you find these chapters informative and also shed illumination on the mystery of that of the Middle Ages. A number of stories took centuries be told since it was not considered to be an important time in history However, it certainly deserves an amount of attention since the colorful times are significant in the books on our history. One of the most surprising aspects in this period is the importance of women in society. They were often portrayed as weak character in earlier times. This isn't the case at all. Queens have made history due to their ability to make smart decisions and the ability to think strategically. Female artisans who were skilled and turned into teachers through the sharing of their craft ran profitable businesses.

The development that the Knight went through was not well-known and many people are shocked to find out how Sir Elton John could be called knight without needing to carry an actual sword. It is also not well-known that the Viking Age, or more specifically, the conclusion of it, is also not popular. It's fascinating to observe how significant religion was in the Middle Ages and how it changed the lives of many people due to their devotion to their religion.